# You're Losing Revenue

Sylvana Seymour

Published by
Goldenlife Circle

Brisbane, Australia



First Edition

ISBN: 978-1-7641980-2-8 (paperback)

ISBN: 978-1-7641980-4-2 (ebook)

Cover design by Sylvana Seymour

# DEDICATION

For those who persist.

# CONTENTS

# INTRODUCTION

Most businesses do not experience a sudden drop in revenue. There is no single moment where something clearly breaks. Enquiries are still coming in, messages are still being answered and some conversations still convert. From the outside, everything appears to be functioning. The pipeline looks active. The activity is there. And yet, the revenue results do not always reflect the level of activity in a consistent way. Some periods perform well. Others fall short without a clear reason. Nothing obvious is missing, but something does not fully add up.

The instinct, when this happens, is to look at the most visible parts of the business. Marketing is reviewed. Pricing is questioned. Individual performance is assessed. Each of these feels like a reasonable place to look because each of them can be observed directly and acted on quickly. They provide a sense of movement at a moment when something feels stuck.

But the source of the problem is rarely in any of those places. It sits somewhere less visible. It sits in the space between an enquiry arriving and a decision being made. In the moments where the conversation was not quite carried forward. In the follow-ups that did not happen. In the next steps that were never defined. In the interactions that simply went quiet and were never revisited.

What is not immediately visible is how many of those enquiries never reach a decision. Conversations begin, develop to a point and then quietly stop. Not because the interest was not real and not because the opportunity was not viable, but because the interaction was not carried through at the right moment or in the right way. No single conversation stands out as a failure. There is no clear point where the revenue was lost. It happens across many interactions, in small, almost unnoticeable ways. And over time, those small losses accumulate into something that is rarely measured, but always felt.

# THE MONTH THAT MADE YOU QUESTION EVERYTHING

There is a month you remember.

Not because it was catastrophic and not because everything fell apart, but because it made no sense.

You did not suddenly forget how to run your business. You did not stop caring. You did not take your foot off the pedal. If anything, you were paying more attention than usual.

And yet, the numbers dropped.

Maybe the month before had been strong. Enquiries coming in. Conversations happening. A few deals closing. Enough to feel like things were working.

Then this month.

Quieter. Slower. Or just... off.

You check everything. Your messages, your pricing, your offer, your own behaviour. You start scanning for the mistake, the thing you must have done wrong.

Because that is where most of us go first.

It must be me.

I am not following up properly. I am not saying the right thing. I am not consistent enough. I am not good at sales.

That thought lands heavier than it should.

Not because it is true, but because it is convincing.

It sounds reasonable. It sounds responsible. It sounds like ownership.

It is also, in most cases, completely wrong.

What you are experiencing in that moment is not a personal failure.

It is not a lack of effort. It is not a lack of ability.

It is a lack of structure.

That is the part almost nobody tells you.

Because the world you are operating in is very quick to make this all about you. Your confidence, your mindset, your tone, your closing technique, your ability to handle objections, build rapport or sell with certainty.

And yes, those things matter.

But they are not the foundation.

You can be excellent at all of them and still have inconsistent revenue. You can be average at all of them and still build a business that produces reliably.

That is the disconnect.

Most conversations about sales are focused on behaviour. Very few are focused on structure.

This book is about structure.

It is not about pushing harder. It is not about becoming someone you are not. It is not about learning a script that makes you sound like every other person in your industry.

It is about understanding how revenue is actually produced inside a business.

Not in theory. Not in a seminar.

In the day-to-day reality of enquiries, conversations and decisions.

Because revenue does not come from effort alone. It comes from a system.

A system that takes a person who shows interest and moves them, step by step, toward a decision.

A system that does not rely on memory, mood or whether you happen to feel "on" that day.

A system that answers one very simple question at every point in time.

What happens next?

When that question is not answered, things drift.

Enquiries come in and then sit. Conversations start and then fade. Follow-ups are remembered sometimes and forgotten other times. Prospects go quiet and you assume they are no longer interested.

Individually, none of these moments feel like a big deal.

Collectively, they are the reason your revenue moves the way it does.

Up one month, down the next, with no clear pattern and no clear cause.

That is the experience this book is here to resolve.

Because once you can see the structure behind your revenue, something shifts.

You stop asking what is wrong with me and start asking what is missing from the process.

You stop relying on motivation and start relying on design.

You stop guessing.

And when you stop guessing, things stabilise.

Not instantly and not magically, but predictably.

That is the goal.

To move you from a place where revenue feels inconsistent and personal to a place where it feels understandable and controllable.

# THERE ARE TWO TYPES OF READER THIS BOOK IS FOR

The first is the business owner who is working hard to bring in new opportunities but does not yet have a clear, repeatable way of moving those opportunities forward. Everything feels manual, effortful and dependent on you being switched on all the time.

The second is the business owner who already has opportunities coming in but can see or at least sense, that value is being lost somewhere along the way. There are conversations that stall, leads that go cold and enquiries that never turn into revenue.

On the surface, these look like different problems.

They are not.

They are the same problem at different stages.

A lack of structure.

Everything that follows in this book is designed to address that.

To show you where the gaps are. To give you a way to measure what your business should be producing, not just what it currently is. And to help you build a system that closes the distance between the two.

You are not bad at sales.

You have been working inside a structure that does not support consistent outcomes.

Once that changes, everything else starts to make more sense.

And more importantly, it starts to work to bring repeatable outcomes in your business.

# PART ONE - THE PROBLEM

## CHAPTER 1
## IT IS NOT YOU

There is a part of running a business that people do not talk about very much. Not publicly, anyway.

It shows up in small moments. Someone asks how things are going and you give a slightly polished version of the truth. Not a lie, just edited. You mention the good parts. You leave out the parts that feel harder to explain. Or you avoid the question altogether.

"How's business?"

"Yeah, good. Busy."

It is easier that way.

Because the honest answer is often more complicated. Some parts are working. Some are not. Some weeks feel productive and others feel like you are pushing against something you cannot quite see. And then there are the numbers. The months that do not match the effort. That is where the discomfort tends to sit.

You know how much time you are putting in. You know how many conversations you are having. You know you are not sitting back waiting for things to happen. And yet the result does not always follow. That gap is difficult to explain, especially to yourself.

So you start to fill it in. Usually with some version of this. 'I should be better at this by now'

It is a quiet thought, but it carries weight. It suggests that the problem is not the business or the market or the way things are set up. It suggests the problem is you. Not skilled enough. Not consistent enough. Not confident enough when it counts. Not good at sales.

That last one tends to land the hardest.

Because sales, whether we like it or not, sits very close to identity when you run a business. It is tied to how you communicate, how you handle pressure and how you respond when someone hesitates or says no. So when revenue is inconsistent it is very easy to interpret that as a reflection of who you are in those moments.

You replay conversations. You think about what you could have said differently. You wonder if you followed up at the right time or if you let something slip. You question whether you are approaching people in the right way at all. It feels like a performance issue. And performance issues feel personal.

The problem is that conclusion is being drawn from incomplete information.

You are looking at an outcome without being able to clearly see the process that created it. When the process is invisible, the only visible variable is you. So the assessment becomes personal by default. But revenue is not created in a single moment of performance. It is not determined by one conversation, one message or one decision point. It is the result of a sequence.

An enquiry comes in. A response is sent. A conversation begins. A next step is suggested. A follow-up happens or it does not. A decision is made, delayed or avoided.

That sequence happens across multiple people, at different stages, at different times. Some of it is handled well. Some of it is delayed. Some of it is missed entirely, not through negligence, but because there is no clear structure holding it all together. When that structure is not defined, outcomes become uneven. Not because you are inconsistent, but because the process is.

You might handle one enquiry quickly and move it forward with clarity. Another comes in on a busy day and sits longer than it should. A conversation progresses well but ends without a clearly defined next step. A prospect goes quiet and is assumed to be no longer interested, even though no real closing point was reached.

Each of these moments is small. None of them feels like a critical mistake. But they accumulate. And when they do they create the exact pattern that leads to that quiet uncomfortable thought ‘I am not good at sales’

It is a convincing conclusion because you can see the outcome. You can feel the inconsistency. You can remember moments where things did not progress. What you cannot easily see is how many of those moments were shaped by the absence of a defined process rather than a lack of ability.

This is where the distinction matters.

A performance problem suggests that you need to improve yourself. Learn more, try harder, adjust how you communicate, become more confident, more persuasive, more consistent. A structural problem suggests something else entirely. It suggests that the way your business handles enquiries and conversations is not designed to produce consistent outcomes, regardless of how capable you are. That is a very different starting point.

Because structure does not rely on personality. It does not depend on whether you are feeling confident that day. It does not require you to remember every follow-up or intuitively guide every conversation to the right place. It creates a path. A defined way for an enquiry to move from initial interest to a decision, with a clear next step at each stage.

When that path exists, your natural ability has somewhere to land. Your effort compounds instead of dispersing. Conversations are less likely to drift because they are not being held together by memory alone.

When that path does not exist, even strong ability produces uneven results.

That is why this matters.

If you misdiagnose the problem as personal, you will keep trying to fix yourself. You will keep adjusting your behaviour, looking for the right words, the right tone, the right approach. And while those things can help at the edges, they do not address the core issue.

The core issue is that there is no consistent structure guiding what happens from one step to the next.

Once you begin to see that, the pressure shifts. Not disappears, but shifts. Away from 'What is wrong with me?' and toward 'How is this process actually working?' That question is far more useful. It opens up something you can examine, adjust and build.

It also sets up everything that follows in this book. Because before you can improve how revenue is produced, you need to understand where it is currently being lost. Not in theory, but in the real, everyday flow of enquiries and conversations that make up your business.

That is where we are going next.

# CHAPTER 2
# THE REVENUE GAP

There is a number sitting inside your business that you have probably never calculated.

Not because it is complex. Not because it requires specialised knowledge. But because no one has ever pointed you toward it in a way that made it feel necessary.

Most business owners track what has already happened. Revenue, expenses, profit, sometimes conversion rates, sometimes average order value. These are useful numbers. They tell you what your business has done. They do not tell you what it should be doing.

That difference matters more than it first appears. Without a reference point, everything feels relative. A good month feels good. A slow month feels concerning. But there is no fixed measure to compare either of them against. So performance becomes something you feel rather than something you can clearly see.

This is where the gap begins.

Every business produces a certain volume of enquiry activity. People who show some level of interest. They make contact, ask questions, request information, begin conversations. That activity has a value. Not theoretical value, not optimistic value, but a grounded measurable value based on what those enquiries would produce if they moved through the business in a consistent way.

Most businesses never calculate that number. Instead they look at what closed. They measure the outcome of what happened rather than the potential of what was already there. So the gap remains invisible.

It sits quietly between the two numbers of what your business is currently producing in revenue and what that same level of enquiry activity could reasonably produce if it were handled in a structured and consistent way.

The before picture is familiar. Enquiries come in and responses are sent. Some conversations continue and others stop without a clear reason. Outcomes vary despite similar activity levels from one month to the next.

The after picture looks different. Enquiries still come in and responses still go out, but each response establishes a next step. Conversations are guided forward deliberately. Pauses are revisited before they become permanent. Outcomes follow a more consistent pattern because the process that produces them is more consistent.

That difference between the two is the revenue gap.

Once you see it, it is difficult to ignore. It reframes everything. A slow month is no longer just a slow month. It becomes a signal that something in the process is not converting as it should. A strong month is no longer just a relief. It becomes a data point showing what is possible when more of the process aligns.

Without that reference it is easy to misread both. You might assume a good month means things are working when in reality it may still be underperforming relative to what is possible. You might assume a slow month means something has gone wrong when in reality it may simply reflect the natural inconsistency of an unstructured process. The gap sits underneath both. Present in each, visible in neither.

It does not announce itself. It does not appear in your accounting software. It does not show up as a line item or surface in most standard reports. You have to calculate it deliberately.

At its simplest it comes down to three inputs: How many enquiries you receive. What those enquiries are worth on average when they convert. And the rate at which they typically convert when handled properly.

That last part is where most businesses hesitate, because conversion is usually thought of as something variable. Something influenced by timing, mood, the quality of the lead, the skill of the person handling the conversation. All of that is true. But within a structured process, conversion tends to fall within a range. Not a fixed number, but a range that is consistent enough to be useful.

Once you realise that, the calculation becomes straightforward.

What is often missing is not the ability to calculate this, but the habit of doing so in a structured way. A certain volume of enquiries, at a certain average value, converting within a reasonable range, produces a predictable revenue output. When your actual revenue sits below that output, the difference is not random. It is the gap. And that gap represents unrealised revenue that has already entered your business in the form of interest.

This is where the discomfort tends to appear, because it challenges a familiar assumption. The assumption that revenue is primarily limited by the number of new enquiries coming in.

In many cases, that is not where the limitation sits.

The limitation sits in how existing enquiries are being handled. Not deliberately, not through lack of care, but through the same absence of structure described in the previous chapter. Without a defined path, some enquiries move forward and others stall. Some are followed up consistently and others are left to memory. Some reach a clear decision point and others fade out without one. Individually each outcome feels situational. Collectively they define the size of the gap.

Once you begin to see your business through that lens, the focus changes. It moves away from trying to generate more activity and toward understanding the value of the activity that is already there.

That does not mean new enquiries are not important. It means they are not the only lever. And in many cases they are not the first one to address, because increasing enquiry volume into an unstructured process often increases the gap rather than closing it. More activity enters the system but the system does not convert it consistently. So the difference between potential and actual widens rather than narrows.

That is why this number matters. It gives you a way to see what your business should be producing, not just what it has produced. It provides a reference point that removes some of the guesswork and creates a foundation for the next step. Because once the gap is visible, the question changes. It is no longer 'How do I get more enquiries?' It becomes 'Where is the value being lost?'

That is what we look at next.

## Why This Is Often Misdiagnosed

Once the gap between enquiry activity and revenue becomes visible, the next question is usually 'Where it is coming from?' At this point most businesses do not immediately look at the structure of their pipeline. They look at the most visible parts of the business instead.

The first conclusion is often that more enquiries are needed. If revenue feels inconsistent, the assumption is that there are not enough opportunities entering the system to produce reliable outcomes. This leads to a focus on marketing, lead generation and increasing visibility. More traffic, more enquiries and more initial conversations are seen as the solution.

This approach is understandable. New enquiries are easy to measure and easy to influence. They provide a clear sense of movement and activity. When more enquiries come in the business feels busier and more engaged. In some cases this does produce an increase in results, at least in the short term.

What it does not address is what happens after those enquiries arrive. If the structure that carries conversations forward is not consistent, increasing the number of enquiries does not resolve the underlying issue. It increases the volume of activity passing through the same process. Some of that activity will convert, but a similar proportion will stall, pause or disappear without reaching a decision. The gap remains. It is simply applied to a larger number of interactions.

Another common conclusion is that the issue sits with individual performance. When outcomes vary it can appear that some conversations are being handled well and others are not. The difference is then attributed to skill, effort or attention. The assumption is that if communication improves, results will stabilise.

There is some truth in this. Individual execution does matter. However when variation is consistent across multiple conversations and over time, it is rarely caused by individual behaviour alone. It is more often a reflection of how the process is structured. Without a defined pipeline even strong communicators produce inconsistent results, because each interaction is handled in isolation. Some progress naturally. Others do not. The outcome depends on the moment rather than the system.

A third explanation is that the market itself has slowed. Demand is seen as weaker, customers are perceived as more hesitant and decisions are thought to be taking longer. In some cases this is accurate. External conditions do change. However this explanation can also obscure what is actually happening inside the business.

When conversations are not being carried through consistently, hesitation becomes more visible. Enquiries appear to stall more often and decisions seem less frequent. This can be interpreted as a change in demand when it is actually a change in how demand is being handled. The same level of interest is present but it is not being converted into decisions at the same rate.

Pricing is another area that is often questioned. If enquiries are coming in but not converting, the assumption may be that the offer is not aligned with what customers are willing to pay. Adjustments are made to pricing, packages or positioning in an attempt to improve outcomes.

This can be relevant in some cases, but it does not explain why conversations are not reaching a decision in the first place. Pricing only becomes a clear factor when a decision point is reached. If interactions are not consistently progressing to that point, changes to pricing will have a limited effect because they are not addressing the stage at which the breakdown is actually occurring.

All of these explanations share a common characteristic. They focus on visible elements of the business. Enquiry volume, individual performance, market conditions and pricing can all be observed directly. They are easier to point to and easier to act on. The structure of the pipeline is less visible. It sits between these elements, shaping how they interact without always being recognised as a separate factor.

This is why the problem is often misdiagnosed. The symptoms are visible but the underlying cause is not immediately apparent. A business may experience inconsistent outcomes and respond by increasing marketing, adjusting pricing or focusing on individual performance. Each of these actions can produce some improvement, but none of them address the core issue if the pipeline itself is not functioning consistently.

When the pipeline is examined directly, a different pattern becomes clear. Enquiries are entering the system but not all of them are being carried forward in a structured way. Conversations begin, develop to a point and then pause. Some are revisited. Others are not. Follow-ups are applied in some cases and missed in others. Next steps are sometimes defined and sometimes left open.

This variation is what creates the gap.

The issue is not that enquiries are missing. It is that progression is inconsistent. The issue is not that conversations are not happening. It is that they are not being carried through to a defined outcome in a reliable way. The issue is not that decisions are not being made. It is that too many interactions never reach the point where a decision can be made at all.

Once this is understood, the earlier explanations can be seen in their proper context. Marketing, performance, market conditions and pricing all influence results, but they operate within the structure of the pipeline. If that structure is weak, their effect is limited. If that structure is strong, their effect is amplified.

This is why the focus shifts from increasing activity to improving movement. The number of enquiries matters, but it is not the primary constraint in many cases. The primary constraint is how those enquiries are handled once they exist.

When that changes, the same level of enquiry activity begins to produce more consistent outcomes. The gap narrows not because more opportunities have been created, but because fewer of the existing ones are being lost along the way.

That is the difference between treating the symptoms and addressing the structure that produces them.

# CHAPTER 3
# WHERE THE MONEY IS LOST

Revenue does not usually disappear in one dramatic moment. There is rarely a single conversation that collapsed, a single follow-up that was missed, a single decision that cost you everything. If it worked that way it would be easier to fix.

What actually happens is quieter and considerably more frustrating. Revenue leaks. Steadily, across a series of small interactions that individually seem fine and collectively explain why the numbers do not add up.

These are not catastrophic failures. They are everyday ones. And because they feel ordinary, they are rarely examined.

One form of loss occurs right at the beginning, before the conversation has properly started. An enquiry comes in and is not responded to quickly or is picked up much later than it should have been. By the time the reply goes out, something has shifted. The person may have moved on, asked elsewhere or simply lost the momentum that prompted them to reach out in the first place. From the business's perspective, the enquiry was received and answered. From the perspective of the person who sent it, the moment has already passed.

This kind of loss leaves almost no trace. There is no rejection, no explicit endpoint and no clear signal that anything went wrong. The conversation simply does not begin. Over the course of a week it might appear minor. Over several months it becomes a pattern, particularly in businesses where response time varies depending on how busy things happen to be that day.

A second form of loss occurs when the response arrives promptly but does not create any movement. The question is answered. The information is provided. The reply is accurate and often quite helpful. What it does not do is establish a next step. So the conversation sits open, waiting for the person on the other end to decide what to do next.

Some will. Particularly those who are already close to a decision and just needed a specific answer before proceeding. But many will not. Not because they lost interest, but because there was no clear reason to act. The enquiry was real. The interest was present. The conversation just did not give them anywhere to go.

This is the one that tends to get misread as a lack of intent. In reality it reflects a lack of structure within the interaction itself.

A third form of loss appears further into the conversation, at a point where things seemed to be going well. An exchange has happened. Some context has been established. The person is engaged. There is genuine momentum. And then the conversation pauses. No follow-up arrives. No next step is introduced. The interaction sits in a kind of limbo, neither active nor finished and quietly fades.

These partially developed conversations represent a particularly sharp form of loss, precisely because they got further than most. More effort went in. More connection was established. There was often a clear indication of interest. And yet they do not reach a conclusion. Over time, they accumulate in the database as the conversations that almost happened. They are, from a purely commercial perspective, the most expensive category of loss, because the investment was made and the return was not.

There is also loss through delay, which is slightly different from absence. The follow-up was intended. The response was drafted in someone's head. The plan was to come back to it. And then something more immediate arrived and pushed it back and then something else did and eventually the moment passed without anyone making a conscious decision to let it go.

These delays are always justified in the moment. There is always something more pressing. But they alter how the pipeline behaves over time. Momentum slows. Continuity breaks. The connection that existed at the last touchpoint begins to weaken. Decisions that might have been reached within a reasonable timeframe become significantly less likely the longer the conversation goes untouched. And the effort required to restart a conversation that has been allowed to cool is almost always greater than the effort that would have been required to maintain it.

Another form of loss and perhaps the most quietly persistent, occurs when conversations are treated as finished simply because they went quiet. The last message was sent. No reply came. So the interaction is filed away as concluded.

In many cases it is not. The person has not necessarily decided against proceeding. They have simply not taken the next step and the conversation was not carried far enough to require one. Without a defined process to revisit it, the interaction sits there, incomplete but no longer considered active. A completed conversation produces a decision. An inactive conversation produces an absence that nobody measures.

What makes all of this particularly tricky is that these patterns do not occur in isolation. They layer. An enquiry might be answered a little late, followed by a response that provides information but no direction, followed by silence that is never revisited. Each stage contributed something small. Together they determined the outcome. From the outside, the business appears to be functioning normally. Enquiries are coming in. Responses are going out. Some conversions are happening. What is not visible is the volume of conversations that started and never finished. They do not register as failures because they were never explicitly lost. They are simply unfinished. And because they do not register as failures, they are not examined. And because they are not examined, they persist in holding revenue.

This is where the revenue gap becomes concrete rather than conceptual. It is not an abstract difference between what could be and what is. It is the cumulative effect of how enquiries are handled at each individual stage. Every passive response, every delayed follow-up, every conversation assumed to be finished when it was actually just quiet, contributes to that gap. None of them look significant on their own. Together they define how much of the available revenue actually gets realised.

Once this is understood, something shifts in how you look at the business. The question stops being how many enquiries are coming in. It becomes how those enquiries are moving once they arrive and where that movement is slowing or stopping.

## How These Losses Appear in Practice

The patterns described above tend to show up in recognisable forms. They do not require unusual circumstances and they are not limited to any particular type of business. They appear wherever enquiries are handled without a consistent structure and they tend to repeat in similar ways regardless of the industry.

At the point of first response, the difference is often small enough to miss entirely. A message is answered, but the reply does not extend beyond what was directly asked. A person enquires about availability or price and receives a direct answer. The information is correct and the response is timely. But the exchange ends at the point of clarification. There is no prompt for continuation and no reason for the person to respond again unless they were already committed to doing so. The conversation appears complete. It has not progressed.

In other cases, the delay is not in whether a response is sent but in when it is sent. An enquiry arrives during a busy period and is answered later in the day or the following morning. The reply still addresses the question, but the context has shifted. The person has either continued their search elsewhere or moved on to other considerations. The interaction is still technically open, but the momentum that would have carried it forward has already dissipated.

A further variation occurs when the conversation begins to develop but loses continuity before it reaches a meaningful next step. There is an exchange of messages. Some context is established. The person responds with additional information. At this point the interaction has moved beyond the initial enquiry and there is a clear opportunity to progress it. Instead the conversation pauses. The next message is not sent or is delayed and the thread sits open without direction. When it is eventually revisited, if it is revisited, the connection that had been established is weaker and the effort required to continue is greater.

These interruptions are most often explained by workload. New enquiries take priority over existing ones, particularly when they are more recent or appear more immediate. The intention to return to earlier conversations remains, but in practice it is frequently deferred. Over time, this creates a pattern where earlier enquiries are less likely to be progressed regardless of how strong their original interest was.

There is also a form of loss that occurs when conversations are treated as complete at the point they go quiet. An enquiry has been answered. There is no further reply. The absence of a response is interpreted as a decision not to proceed and the interaction is left as it is. In many cases that assumption is never tested. The conversation is not revisited. No further attempt is made to clarify whether a decision has actually been reached.

From the perspective of the person who made the enquiry, the situation may look quite different. They may still be considering their options. They may have intended to come back to the conversation. They may simply need further clarification before they can move forward. Without a prompt from the business, however, the interaction remains inactive. And the difference between inactivity and completion is not always visible. Without a defined process, it is not consistently addressed.

These patterns can also be observed across longer timeframes in ways that make their cumulative effect harder to ignore. Over the course of a week, a number of enquiries are received and responded to. Some convert. Others do not. The outcome appears mixed but not unusual. Over the course of a month, the same pattern repeats. A proportion of enquiries progress while others remain incomplete. The volume of activity is consistent, but the proportion that reaches a decision does not increase.

Over several months, the picture becomes clearer and less comfortable. A significant number of enquiries have passed through the business without reaching a defined outcome. They are not recorded as lost opportunities, because they were never explicitly declined. They are simply absent from the final results. The business continues to generate revenue, but the relationship between the effort that went in and the outcomes that came out remains murky.

This is where the distinction between activity and progression becomes important. Activity refers to the number of enquiries received and the number of responses sent. Progression refers to how those enquiries actually move through the interaction toward a decision. It is entirely possible for activity to remain high while progression remains inconsistent. When that happens, the business appears busy. The underlying flow is anything but.

When viewed through this lens, the sources of loss become easier to locate. They are not concentrated in a single point. They are distributed across the interaction. A response that does not guide. A delay that reduces momentum. A conversation that is not revisited. An assumption that something is finished when it is actually just quiet. Each one is small. Together they define the gap between what is possible and what is actually achieved.

Time and Accumulation

The effect of these patterns is rarely immediate. In most cases the difference between a structured and an unstructured approach is not visible within a single day. It becomes clearer over time, which is part of why it is so easy to overlook until it has been building for months.

On the first day, the difference may appear minimal. Enquiries are received, responses are sent and some conversations begin to develop. On the second or third day, the difference begins to emerge. Some conversations have progressed to a defined next step while others have paused. The distinction is still subtle and may not be immediately recognisable as anything significant.

Over the course of a week, the pattern becomes more apparent. Conversations that were guided continue to move forward. Those that were left open begin to fall out of view. Follow-ups that were completed maintain their stopped status. Those that were delayed require more effort to resume. The number of active conversations may look similar, but their distribution has quietly changed.

Over a longer period, the cumulative effect becomes difficult to ignore. A structured approach produces a higher proportion of conversations that reach a decision, even when the number of enquiries remains exactly the same. An unstructured approach produces a higher proportion of conversations that remain incomplete. The difference is not in the level of demand coming in. It is in how that demand is handled once it arrives.

This accumulation is what defines the revenue gap in practical terms. It is not the result of one missed opportunity. It is the result of repeated patterns that influence how enquiries move over time, compounding quietly in the background while the business focuses on whatever is most visible that day.

Once this is understood, the focus shifts from individual outcomes to the consistency of the process that produces them. The question is no longer what happened in this particular conversation. It is what is happening across all of them.

To answer that, you need to look at the path enquiries actually follow. Which means understanding what a pipeline actually is, in terms that are useful in practice rather than as a general concept that sounds good in a business conversation.

That is where we go next.

# CHAPTER 4
# WHAT A PIPELINE ACTUALLY IS

The word pipeline gets used a lot in business. It appears in conversations about growth, in advice about sales, in almost every discussion about how businesses should be managing their opportunities. And yet, despite how often it comes up, it is rarely defined in a way that actually makes it useful.

For most business owners, it ends up meaning one of two things. Either a list of people they have spoken to or a vague sense of how opportunities tend to move from first contact toward a decision at some point. Neither of these is quite accurate. A pipeline is not a list. It is a path.

More specifically, it is a defined path that an enquiry follows from the moment it enters your business to the point where a decision is made. That path is made up of stages and each stage has a purpose. Movement through those stages is not left to chance or memory or whoever happens to have bandwidth that afternoon. It is guided.

When a pipeline is not defined, the path still exists. It just lives informally, in the heads of the people managing the conversations, changing shape depending on the situation, the day and how much attention each interaction happens to receive. Some enquiries move forward smoothly. Others stall. Some are followed up consistently. Others are not. The experience varies, not because the people involved are different in any meaningful way, but because the process is not fixed.

When a pipeline is defined, that variability begins to reduce. Each enquiry enters at a known point and moves through a sequence of stages that are clearly understood. At each stage, there is an expected next step and the responsibility for that step is clear. Movement from one stage to the next becomes intentional rather than accidental.

This does not make the process rigid. It makes it visible. And that distinction matters more than it might first appear. A rigid process forces conversations into a structure that does not fit them. A visible process provides a structure that supports them. It gives shape to something that would otherwise rely entirely on memory and timing and the particular mood of whoever is handling the inbox that day.

From the outside, the difference is not always obvious. Conversations still happen. Questions are still answered. Decisions are still made. From the inside, the experience changes considerably.

Without a defined pipeline, each conversation requires you to decide what to do next in the moment. You are reading the situation, assessing the person, forming a response and trying to move things forward, all at the same time, with no fixed reference point. A response at this stage often looks something like this.

"Hi, yes we have a few options available. Let me know what you're after."

The person reads that. There is a brief pause. Nothing has been decided yet, but a small evaluation is already taking place. The response answered the question, but it has also introduced a kind of direction. The question now is whether it feels easy to continue.

This moment is rarely visible from inside the business. But it is precisely where many conversations either progress or quietly stop.

With a defined pipeline, much of that in-the-moment decision making is already done before the conversation begins. The same interaction, handled within a defined structure, tends to look a little different.

"Hi, yes we have a few options in that range. Are you looking for something simple or something more detailed? I can send through a couple of examples."

The next step is not something that had to be invented on the spot. It is something that is applied. This reduces friction on both sides. It also changes how you see the flow of your business more broadly. Instead of a series of separate, disconnected interactions that you are managing individually, you begin to see a progression. Enquiries enter. They move through stages. They exit as either decisions or non-decisions. The movement becomes easier to follow and, more importantly, easier to influence.

This is where the connection to the previous chapters becomes clear. The revenue gap described earlier is not created randomly. It is created at specific points where that movement breaks down. Where an enquiry does not progress as it could. Where a stage is unclear. Where a next step is missing. A defined pipeline makes those points visible. It allows you to see where enquiries are sitting, how long they have been there and what is supposed to happen next. It gives you a way to understand the flow rather than guess at it.

### What This Looks Like Day to Day

In practice, working with a defined pipeline often involves reviewing a small number of enquiries at different points throughout the day. Not a lengthy process. Not a complicated system. Just a consistent habit of checking where things are and what needs to happen next.

New enquiries are checked and responded to. Existing conversations are revisited to confirm their current stage. Where a next step has not yet been taken, that becomes visible rather than being left to the chance of someone remembering.

Some enquiries move forward immediately. Others remain in place for a period of time. The difference is that they are seen, rather than left to drift in the background of a busy inbox.

Importantly, a pipeline is not just a tracking tool. It is a behavioural guide. If a stage is defined but there is no clear next step attached to it, the pipeline is incomplete. If a next step exists but is not consistently applied, the pipeline is not functioning as intended. The value comes from the combination of definition and consistent use. One without the other produces a system that looks organised but does not actually change anything.

This is where many attempts to build a pipeline fall short. The structure is created, often inside a CRM or a spreadsheet and it is set up with good intentions. But it remains separate from the actual conversations. It records what has happened without influencing what happens next. A working pipeline does both. It reflects the current position of each enquiry and directs the next action that should be taken. It sits alongside the conversations, not behind.

Once this is genuinely in place, the experience of managing enquiries begins to change in ways that are difficult to describe until you have felt them. You are no longer relying on memory to keep track of who needs to be contacted. You are not scanning through messages trying to work out where things stand. You are not deciding from scratch how to move each conversation forward. The structure carries that weight. Your role becomes one of applying it consistently rather than reinventing it daily.

This is why a pipeline actually matters. Not as a piece of business terminology. Not as a system for the sake of being organised. But as the mechanism through which enquiry activity is turned into revenue in a consistent way. Without it, outcomes vary and the variation is largely invisible. With it, outcomes begin to stabilise and the reasons for any variation become easier to identify and address.

The next step is to define what that pipeline should look like for your specific business. Which means understanding what the stages actually are, how many you need and what distinguishes one from another.

That is what the next chapter is about.

# CHAPTER 5
# WHO BELONGS IN YOUR PIPELINE

The instinct, when building a pipeline, is to put everyone in it.

Anyone who makes contact, asks a question or expresses any level of interest gets added to the list. On the surface this seems reasonable. If someone has reached out, they represent potential. And potential is what the pipeline is designed to capture. So in they go.

The problem is that not every interaction functions in the same way. Not every enquiry contributes equally to movement through the pipeline. Some represent clear intent. Others reflect early-stage curiosity. Some are specific and actionable. Others are vague and exploratory. Treating all of them as equivalent does not make the pipeline more comprehensive. It makes it harder to read.

The question worth asking is not simply who has made contact. It is who can actually be carried through the process in a meaningful way. In practical terms, an enquiry belongs in the pipeline when it is capable of progression. Not simply because contact has been made, but because the interaction can move forward through a defined sequence toward a decision.

At the point of entry, most enquiries look similar. A message is received, a question is asked and a response is required. The distinction between different types of enquiries is not always obvious at this stage. It tends to become clearer as the conversation develops and the person's intent begins to show itself.

Some enquiries arrive with a defined purpose. The person has a specific question, a clear requirement or an immediate need. These interactions tend to progress more directly. They move from initial contact toward a next step with relatively little resistance. The pipeline's job here is to support that movement and make sure it is not interrupted by delays or passive responses.

Other enquiries arrive without that level of clarity. The person may be unsure of what they need or is gathering information before making a decision. These interactions require more development.

They do not move forward on their own. They need to be guided through a process that establishes context and gradually introduces a path toward a decision.

Both types belong in the pipeline. But they do not behave in the same way and treating them as identical tends to produce inconsistent handling. Clear enquiries may be slowed by unnecessary steps. Uncertain enquiries may be left without sufficient direction. Understanding the difference from early in the conversation allows you to apply the right approach rather than the same approach to everyone.

## Activity Is Not the Same as Progression

There is also a category of interaction that sits at the edge of the pipeline and this one is worth being honest about.

These are enquiries that do not progress beyond an initial exchange. A single question. A brief message. A request that generates a response but then produces nothing further. In some cases this reflects a genuine lack of intent. In others it reflects a lack of engagement within the interaction itself, where the response did not create enough reason to continue.

Deciding whether these belong in the pipeline requires a distinction between activity and progression. Activity refers to the fact that contact has been made. Progression refers to whether that contact can be developed into a structured interaction moving toward a decision. Not all activity leads to progression and not all activity should be treated as part of the working pipeline.

This does not mean low-engagement enquiries should be ignored or dismissed. They should still be responded to and handled appropriately. The difference lies in how they are categorised. Including them alongside actively developing conversations creates noise. It becomes more difficult to see which enquiries are genuinely moving forward and which have effectively already stopped.

A similar consideration applies to repeat enquiries. These may come from the same person over time, often with variations of the same question asked in slightly different ways. In some cases this indicates ongoing interest that just needs more time or more information to convert. In others it reflects hesitation or an inability to move beyond the initial stage for reasons that have not yet been surfaced.

Treating each instance as a separate opportunity can inflate the apparent volume of the pipeline without actually increasing the likelihood of any of it progressing. When viewed as part of a single, ongoing interaction rather than a series of new ones, repeat enquiries can provide genuinely useful information. They show where the conversation keeps returning to the same point, which is usually a signal that something needs to be addressed more directly before movement is possible.

There are also enquiries that are technically valid but simply not aligned with what the business offers. Requests that fall outside the scope of what is available. Expectations that cannot be met. Situations where the fit is not appropriate regardless of how the conversation develops. Including these in the pipeline creates false signals. They occupy space within the process but they are unlikely to reach a meaningful outcome and they dilute attention from the enquiries that could.

Excluding them does not mean dismissing them without response. It means recognising that they do not belong within the structured path that leads to a decision. They are handled, but they are not carried through the same sequence as enquiries that are genuinely aligned.

## How Behaviour Diverges Over Time

The distinction between different types of enquiries is not always obvious at the point of entry. It becomes considerably clearer when viewed over time.

On the first day, most enquiries do appear similar. A message is received, a response is sent and the interaction begins. At this stage it is genuinely not always obvious which conversations will progress and which will not.

By the second or third day, patterns begin to emerge. Some enquiries continue to develop. The person responds, provides more information and engages with the direction the conversation is taking. Other enquiries remain unchanged. They have been answered, but nothing further has happened and nothing further seems likely to.

Over the course of a week, this separation becomes more pronounced. Enquiries that are capable of progression move into later stages. They reach points where a next step is introduced and in some cases accepted. Enquiries that are not progressing remain in earlier stages or fall out of view entirely, which is a different thing from being resolved.

Without a defined boundary between these two categories, both types remain grouped together. The pipeline appears full, but the movement within it is uneven. Some conversations are genuinely advancing. Others are static. And from a distance they can look identical.

Over a longer period, this has a cumulative effect that is worth understanding clearly. A pipeline that includes all enquiries regardless of their likelihood to progress will continue to grow in volume over time, but not necessarily in outcomes. A pipeline that focuses on progressing enquiries will show more consistent movement, even if the total number of enquiries within it appears lower. This is not a difference in demand. It is a difference in how demand is being defined and managed.

## When It Is Not Clear Who Belongs

When the boundary is not maintained clearly, the behaviour of the whole system begins to change in ways that are subtle but significant.

One effect is that attention gets distributed across all enquiries regardless of their likelihood to progress. Time is spent responding to, revisiting and managing interactions that are not moving forward in any meaningful way. Meanwhile, enquiries that are genuinely developing may not receive the level of attention required to maintain their momentum. This is a form of dilution that rarely announces itself. It just quietly lowers the overall effectiveness of time spent.

Another effect is that the pipeline becomes harder to interpret. A large number of enquiries may be present, but it is not clear how many of them are active in any practical sense. The distinction between an enquiry that is progressing and one that has stopped blurs. Decisions about where to focus, which conversations to prioritise and where the process is working or failing become harder to make with any confidence. The pipeline appears to contain information, but that information is less useful than it looks.

Over time, this can lead to a reliance on feeling rather than observation. The pipeline feels busy. But the underlying movement is not fully understood and adjustments get made based on general impressions rather than specific patterns that can actually be acted on.

## Re-Entry

Not all enquiries follow a single, uninterrupted path through the pipeline.

Some leave and return. A person makes an initial enquiry, does not proceed and then re-engages weeks or months later. The question in these cases is not whether the enquiry is new, but whether it is a continuation of a previous interaction.

Treating it as new creates unnecessary duplication. The context that was previously established gets ignored and the conversation starts again from the beginning. This can feel like a repetitive slap in the face to the person on the other end and it loses the advantage of what was already built.

Treating it as a continuation allows the interaction to resume from where it left off. Prior context can be referenced. The conversation can move forward more efficiently. And the person receives the implicit message that they were remembered, which is exactly what you're aiming for in a sales context.

## When It Stops Belonging

Inclusion in the pipeline is not a permanent condition.

An enquiry may enter the pipeline, develop to a point and then cease to progress. This does not always mean it should remain there indefinitely. At a certain point, it becomes necessary to make an honest assessment of whether further movement is likely without some significant change in circumstances.

This is not a rigid threshold and there is no universal rule for when to make that call. It is based on the pattern of the interaction. A conversation that has been revisited multiple times without producing any response may no longer be active in any practical sense. A conversation that has paused after reaching a defined next step may still be relevant and worth maintaining.

The distinction lies in whether the interaction can realistically be progressed through the existing process. If it cannot, it may need to be removed from the active pipeline and treated differently. This does not mean discarding them entirely. They may be revisited at a later point or re-enter the pipeline under different conditions. The point is simply that that activity should not be treated as part of the current flow when it is not moving.

Maintaining this boundary prevents the pipeline from becoming a historical record of everything that ever happened rather than a live representation of what is currently in motion. And a pipeline that reflects history only rather than progression is not really doing its job.

## Clarity Creates Focus

When the pipeline contains only those enquiries that are genuinely capable of progression, something useful happens. It becomes easier to understand how the process is actually functioning. Movement between stages can be observed more clearly. Areas of friction become easier to identify. Effort can be directed toward the conversations that are most likely to produce an outcome rather than spread evenly across everything.

Without this distinction, the pipeline becomes a record of all activity rather than a representation of active progression. It may appear full, but that fullness does not translate into movement. Conversations that are not advancing sit alongside conversations that are and the difference between them is less visible than it should be.

This clarity also allows for a more accurate understanding of performance over time. The proportion of enquiries that progress can be measured against a defined set rather than a broad, undifferentiated collection of activity. This makes it easier to identify where improvements can be made and where the process is already functioning as it should.

Over a longer timeframe, the difference between a pipeline that includes all activity and one that focuses on progression becomes increasingly significant. The former may always appear busy. The latter will consistently produce more reliable outcomes.

The effectiveness of the system depends on that distinction being maintained, not once at the beginning when the pipeline is first built, but consistently over time as new enquiries arrive and old ones reach their natural conclusion.

Once that boundary is established and maintained, the pipeline becomes a genuinely useful tool rather than an overgrown contact list with stages attached to it.

Which brings the focus to what those stages should actually look like. How they are defined, how many there should be and what distinguishes one from another in a way that is practical enough to use consistently.

That is what the next chapter is about.

# CHAPTER 6
# BUILDING THE STAGES

Once the idea of a pipeline is understood, the next question is how the path is actually defined. It is one thing to recognise that enquiries move through a sequence. It is another to make that sequence visible in a way that can be applied consistently across different conversations, different days and different levels of busyness.

In many businesses, stages exist informally. There is a sense of progression, a general feeling that things move from enquiry to conversation to decision at some point, but it is not clearly defined. An enquiry is received, a conversation begins and at some point a decision is made. The steps in between are understood in general terms but not structured in a way that can be observed or repeated. This means that while movement does occur, it is not always clear where it is happening or where it is quietly slowing down.

Defining the stages makes that progression explicit. It turns what is assumed into something that can actually be seen and worked with. Each stage represents a point in the conversation where something specific is happening. Not in a vague sense, but in a way that can be recognised across multiple interactions and applied consistently. This allows different conversations to be compared, not by their content or tone, but by their position within the process.

At a simple level, most pipelines follow a similar pattern. An enquiry enters, the conversation develops, a next step is introduced and a decision is reached. This sequence appears straightforward. In practice, without clear definition, it becomes inconsistent. Conversations move at different speeds, skip steps or stall without any obvious reason. What looks like variation in outcomes is often just variation in how consistently the sequence is being applied.

The purpose of defining stages is not to force every interaction into a rigid structure that overrides the natural flow of a conversation. It is to create a shared reference point that allows movement to be understood. When each stage has a clear purpose, it becomes easier to see whether an enquiry is progressing as expected or beginning to slow. This shifts the focus from reacting to individual conversations to observing the flow between stages, which is a considerably more useful place to be.

Most pipelines can be described using a small number of core stages. They do not need to be complex. In fact, simplicity is an asset here, because simple stages are easier to apply consistently. A typical structure might include the initial enquiry, the first response, the development of the conversation, the introduction of a next step and the movement toward a decision. The labels themselves matter less than the clarity they create around what is actually happening at each point.

When stages are not defined, the pipeline loses visibility in ways that compound over time. An enquiry is received and answered and at that moment it appears to have been handled. If there is no reply, the interaction fades into the background. There is no clear distinction between an enquiry that has been answered and is actively progressing and one that has effectively stopped. Both appear complete in the moment, even though one is still in motion and the other has quietly ceased to be. This creates a false sense of completion, where activity is recorded but progression is not.

The absence of defined stages also affects behaviour in a subtler way. Without a clear understanding of where an enquiry sits, the next step tends to be decided on the fly. Some conversations are guided forward with intention. Others are left open because the right next move was not obvious in the moment. The difference is not deliberate. It is simply the result of not having a consistent reference point to work from. Over time, these small variations accumulate and create uneven movement across the pipeline.

When stages are defined clearly, the same interactions begin to look different. An enquiry is no longer simply answered. It is moved from one stage to another. A conversation is no longer simply ongoing. It is either progressing or it is not and that distinction is visible. This makes movement observable. It becomes possible to see where enquiries are sitting, how long they have been there and what should be happening next.

This visibility allows patterns to emerge that would otherwise remain hidden. Certain stages may consistently contain more enquiries than others. Some stages may show steady movement while others become the points where conversations regularly slow or stop. Instead of relying on a general impression of how things are going, the pipeline begins to provide specific, observable signals about where attention is needed.

## What Ineffective Stage Design Looks Like

It is possible to have stages defined and still have a pipeline that does not function well in practice. Understanding what goes wrong is as useful as understanding what to aim for.

One common problem is that everything effectively sits in a single stage. A business may technically define multiple stages, but in day-to-day use most enquiries are treated the same way. They are received, responded to and then left in a general category labelled something like active or in progress. Because there is no meaningful distinction being made between stages in practice, movement cannot be observed. Conversations that are developing and conversations that have stalled appear identical. The pipeline becomes a list rather than a system and a list is significantly less useful.

This creates a situation where activity is visible but progression is not. The business can see how many enquiries exist but not how many are actually moving forward. As a result, attention is not directed effectively. Time may be spent on conversations that are not progressing while those that require a next step are overlooked.

Another common issue is the opposite problem and it is equally unhelpful in practice. In an attempt to capture every possible variation in the sales process, too many stages get defined. Each small shift in the conversation is given its own label. While this might appear thorough, it reduces usability considerably. If a stage cannot be easily recognised in practice, it will not be applied consistently. The result is hesitation. Instead of moving enquiries forward with confidence, time gets spent deciding where they belong.

This leads to a form of paralysis. The pipeline becomes difficult to use, so it is used less. Stages get skipped, combined or quietly ignored. The structure exists in theory but not in practice. The intention was to create clarity, but the result is increased friction.

A third issue arises when stages are defined correctly but not followed consistently. This tends to show up as stage skipping, where a conversation moves from initial enquiry directly toward a decision without passing through the intermediate stages in a structured way. In some cases this is entirely appropriate. A strong enquiry from someone who is ready to move quickly does not need to be slowed down by unnecessary steps. The problem arises when skipping stages becomes the default behaviour rather than the exception.

When that happens, the pipeline loses its ability to provide meaningful signals. It becomes difficult to identify where conversations are slowing because the intermediate steps are not being observed. Some enquiries will still convert, but the overall system becomes less predictable and less manageable. The structure is present but it is not being used to guide behaviour.

There is also a more subtle version of this, where conversations appear to move through the stages but without completing the purpose of each one. A consultation might be introduced before sufficient context has been established. Options might be presented before the person's preferences are clearly understood. The stage is technically reached, but its function has not been fulfilled. This weakens everything that follows, because later stages in the pipeline rely on what should have been established earlier.

These issues are not always obvious because the pipeline may still produce results. Some enquiries will progress regardless of how well the structure is applied. The effect of poor stage design is not that nothing works. It is that outcomes become inconsistent. Some conversations move smoothly while others stall without a clear reason and the reason for the difference is not visible.

The practical effect of stage definition becomes considerably clearer when considered across different types of businesses, because the stages themselves look different depending on the context, even though the underlying principle remains the same.

In a jewellery setting, the sequence tends to follow a relatively direct path. An enquiry arrives asking about a piece, a style or a price range. The initial response acknowledges the request and introduces direction, often by asking a clarifying question about what the person is looking for. As the conversation develops, preferences become clearer and options are presented. A next step is introduced, such as viewing the piece in person, reserving it or reviewing alternatives. From there the interaction moves toward a decision.

When this sequence is defined, it becomes easier to see where movement is occurring and where it is not. A common point of delay tends to appear after options have been sent. The enquiry has moved beyond the initial stage, but the next step has not yet been secured. Without a defined stage for this moment, it can easily be overlooked as simply part of an ongoing conversation. With a defined stage, it becomes clear that the conversation is waiting to be progressed and that waiting is something that requires action rather than patience.

In a hair clinic, the stages often involve more uncertainty at the beginning than in other categories. An enquiry may start with a general question about thinning, hair loss or treatment suitability rather than a clear request for a specific service. The initial response needs to do more than confirm that treatment exists. It needs to begin defining the situation. As the conversation develops, more context is established around what the person is experiencing and what they are trying to understand. A consultation is then introduced as the natural next step and the interaction moves toward booking, attending and deciding.

Here the stages are less about selecting an option and more about building clarity over time. Without clear definition, these interactions can sit in an early stage for longer than expected. The conversation appears active but it is not actually progressing toward a decision. Defining the stages makes that distinction visible. It becomes clearer whether the interaction has genuinely moved from initial enquiry to developing context and from there to a consultation stage or whether it has been sitting in the same place for longer than it should have been.

In a med spa setting, the stages often begin with a treatment question that appears simple on the surface but carries a second layer of uncertainty underneath it. A person may ask about lip filler, a skin treatment or another procedure in a way that sounds as though they are only asking about price. In practice, the enquiry often includes unspoken questions about outcome, suitability and level of commitment. The initial response therefore needs to introduce context alongside the direct answer. As the conversation develops, the desired result becomes clearer and a consultation is introduced as the next step. From there the enquiry moves toward booking, attending and deciding.

A common point of delay in this sequence occurs after the consultation is introduced. At that point the interaction shifts from discussion to commitment and that shift often produces hesitation that can be difficult to read accurately. Without a defined stage for that moment, the hesitation can easily be misread as a loss of interest and the conversation can be left to fade. With a defined stage, it becomes easier to recognise that the conversation is still active but sitting at a specific point where it needs a particular kind of attention before it can progress.

In a cosmetic dental setting, the stages extend further because the decision carries considerably more weight. An enquiry may begin with a question about veneers, aligners or cosmetic treatment pricing, but the underlying issue is rarely cost alone. The person is trying to understand what is possible, what the treatment would involve and whether the outcome justifies the commitment. The initial response therefore introduces context around the desired outcome rather than moving directly to consultation. As the conversation develops, a clearer picture of the person's goals is established. A consultation is introduced and the interaction moves toward booking, attending, planning and deciding.

In these higher-value interactions, the decision stage often lasts longer than in other categories. After the consultation, the conversation may pause while the person considers cost, timing and the significance of what they are committing to. Without a defined stage for this period, the interaction can appear inactive when it is actually still in motion. With a defined stage, it remains part of the pipeline and can be managed accordingly. The role of the structure is not to force the decision. It is to keep the interaction visible until a defined outcome is actually reached.

Across all four examples, the stages are not identical. The content of each conversation, the pace of progression and the points of natural hesitation are all different. But the principle remains constant. Each stage represents a point where the conversation changes in a meaningful way. The purpose of defining them is not to categorise interactions for the sake of organisation, but to make movement visible so that it can be influenced.

When movement is visible, it becomes easier to influence. Delays can be identified before they become permanent. Patterns can be observed and adjustments can be made with more precision rather than based on a general feeling that something somewhere is not quite working. Without that visibility, the pipeline relies on perception. Some conversations feel active and others do not, but the reasons are not always clear and the response is not always targeted.

The goal is not a perfect model. It is a usable one. Something that can be applied across different types of enquiries without requiring constant interpretation or recalibration. Once the stages are defined in a way that is both meaningful and practical, the pipeline begins to take shape and enquiry activity becomes something that can be observed and managed rather than simply experienced and hoped for.

At that point the focus shifts again. It is no longer about defining where conversations sit. It is about how they move between those positions. The stages define the structure. The messaging determines whether anything actually moves.

That is what we look at next.

# CHAPTER 7
# THE MESSAGING THAT MOVES PEOPLE FORWARD

Once the stages of a pipeline are defined, a different question begins to take shape. It is no longer enough to understand where a conversation sits. The focus shifts to what is actually said at each point and how that communication influences whether the interaction continues to move or quietly settles into inactivity.

Many businesses do not immediately recognise this as a separate issue, because communication is already taking place. Messages are being sent, questions are being answered and information is being shared. From a surface perspective, nothing appears to be missing. The interaction exists and is active in the moment. The difficulty lies in what that interaction is actually doing. More often than not, it is maintaining contact without creating movement.

A conversation can continue for quite some time in this way. A prospect asks a question and receives a response. They reply and another response follows. The exchange feels engaged. The direction, however, remains unclear. At some point the interaction begins to slow. At some point it stops. There is no clear error and no single moment where anything obviously fails. The conversation simply does not progress to a defined outcome and the reason is not visible from inside the individual messages.

This is where messaging takes on a more specific role. It is not about refining wording or making responses sound more persuasive. It is about understanding what each message is intended to do within the structure of the pipeline. When the stages are defined, each point in the conversation carries a different requirement. The messaging needs to align with that requirement if movement is going to occur consistently rather than occasionally.

At the beginning of an interaction, the purpose of communication is not only to acknowledge the enquiry but to establish direction. A response that confirms capability without introducing a next step leaves the conversation open in a way that requires the other person to figure out what happens next. A reply such as "yes, we can help with that" is accurate and entirely appropriate in tone. But it does not create forward movement. The interaction remains dependent on the other person deciding what to do, which is a dependency you want to reduce rather than increase.

At the other extreme, an overly forceful response attempts to move too quickly. Something like "we can book you in tomorrow at 10am or 2pm, which works for you" may create pressure before sufficient context has been established. In some cases this produces resistance rather than progress. The conversation has been pushed beyond the point it has actually reached and the person on the other end can feel that.

Somewhere between these two positions is the more effective approach. A response that introduces direction without forcing a decision tends to create movement without friction. Asking whether the person is looking to proceed soon or is still exploring options establishes context while keeping the interaction open. The conversation moves forward because the next step has been made visible, not because it has been imposed.

The distinction at this stage is subtle but worth understanding clearly. Passive messaging stabilises the conversation without advancing it. Overly forceful messaging disrupts it. Directed messaging carries it forward. Only one of those three is doing what you actually need it to do.

As the conversation progresses, the role of messaging changes again. Once an initial connection has been established, the focus moves toward understanding what sits behind the enquiry. At this stage, the quality of the interaction depends less on the information provided and more on how effectively the underlying situation is defined.

A broad question such as "what are you looking for" keeps the conversation active, but it often produces a response that lacks useful clarity. The person may answer in general terms, which makes it difficult to determine what should happen next. At the other extreme, a question that is too narrow can restrict the interaction before sufficient context has been developed.

A more directed approach introduces context without limiting the response. Asking what prompted the enquiry or what has led the person to explore the option tends to produce more useful information. It moves the conversation from surface-level detail to underlying intent. This shift is not dramatic from the outside, but it changes what becomes possible in the later stages of the interaction considerably.

This stage requires judgement. The balance between open and directed questioning depends on how the other person is engaging and what has already been established. Too little direction results in vague responses that cannot be progressed. Too much direction can close down the conversation before it has developed enough to be useful. The purpose is not to control the interaction. It is to guide it toward clarity, which is a different thing altogether.

Once the conversation reaches a point where the situation is genuinely understood, messaging takes on a different function. It becomes responsible for guiding the interaction toward a defined next step. This is where the contrast between passive, forceful and directed communication becomes most visible in practice.

A passive approach leaves the next step undefined. A message such as "let me know if you would like to go ahead" appears perfectly reasonable, but it places the entire burden of action on the other person. Even when interest is genuinely present, this often results in inaction. The path forward requires effort to determine and that effort is often just enough to prevent the step from being taken.

A forceful approach attempts to remove that uncertainty by pushing for a decision before the conversation is ready for one. A message such as "I'll book you in for Thursday unless I hear otherwise" creates urgency, but it can also create resistance if the conversation has not actually reached that point. The interaction may move forward in some cases, but it does so at the risk of damaging the engagement that made it possible in the first place.

A directed approach introduces a clear next step while allowing the other person to engage with it on their own terms. Offering two possible time frames for a meeting or suggesting a specific way to proceed reduces the effort required to act. The decision becomes easier because the options are visible. The conversation moves forward because the path has been made clear, not because pressure has been applied.

This distinction becomes even more important when hesitation appears, which it will at some point in almost every substantive conversation.

Hesitation tends to be interpreted as a negative signal. A delayed response, a vague reply or a pause in communication is commonly read as a loss of interest. In practice, hesitation is more often a point of evaluation. The person is not disengaging. They are deciding. And there is a significant difference between those two states, even though from the outside they can look identical.

Price is a common source of hesitation. When a cost is introduced, the conversation may slow noticeably. This is often interpreted as rejection. In many cases it is a sign that the person is assessing value rather than withdrawing interest. A passive response at this point or no response at all, allows the conversation to stop when it was actually still in motion. A forceful response that immediately attempts to justify the price can create pressure at exactly the wrong moment.

A more effective approach is to reintroduce context. Clarifying what the price relates to or how the outcome is defined helps the person continue their evaluation. The purpose is not to persuade. It is to make the decision easier to process. When this is handled well, the conversation remains active rather than collapsing into a silence that gets misread as a conclusion.

Timing hesitation follows a similar pattern. A person may express genuine interest but indicate that they are not ready to proceed immediately. This is often treated as a low-priority interaction and left to sit. In reality it represents a conversation that has reached a specific point where timing needs to be managed rather than ignored.

A passive response allows the interaction to drift until it disappears entirely. A forceful response attempts to accelerate a decision that is not yet ready to be made. A directed response acknowledges the timing and maintains continuity. Suggesting a point to reconnect or keeping the conversation open with a defined next step ensures that the interaction does not simply evaporate because it was not immediate.

What is often described as ghosting falls into a similar category. A conversation that was active suddenly goes quiet. The assumption is that the person has decided not to proceed. In some cases that is true. In many cases it is not. The absence of a reply is not always a decision. It is often a pause that simply has not been addressed.

How this is handled determines whether the interaction can be recovered. A passive approach accepts the silence as an endpoint. A forceful approach attempts to force a response, which tends to produce either resistance or further silence. A directed approach reconnects to the existing conversation, referencing what has already been discussed and reintroducing a clear path forward. This reduces the effort required to respond. When that connection is maintained, re-engagement becomes much easier. When the connection is lost, the conversation effectively resets and the likelihood that it will continue drops considerably.

These patterns repeat across the pipeline in consistent and recognisable ways. Messages that answer without directing, messages that inform without guiding and messages that fail to adapt when the conversation changes all contribute to the same outcome. Each one appears reasonable when viewed in isolation. When repeated across many interactions over time, they create a consistent reduction in movement that shows up in the numbers without a clear explanation being visible in any individual conversation.

This is why messaging cannot be separated from structure. The stages define where the conversation sits. The messaging determines whether it moves. When the two are not aligned, outcomes become inconsistent. Some interactions progress because the messaging happens to match the moment. Others do not. The difference is not always visible at the level of individual conversations, but it becomes clear when viewed across the pipeline as a whole.

Once the stages are clearly defined, messaging can be aligned to them in a more deliberate way. Each stage has a purpose and each purpose requires a specific type of communication. This is not a matter of scripting responses word for word. It is a matter of understanding direction. Messages that are intentional in this sense do more than respond to what has been said. They shape what happens next.

When this alignment is applied consistently, conversations begin to change in character. They move with greater clarity and reach defined points more reliably. The likelihood of interactions stalling without explanation is reduced. This does not happen because the wording has become more persuasive. It happens because the messaging is performing its actual role within the structure of the pipeline rather than just filling the space between one exchange and the next.

That alignment is what allows the pipeline to function as a system rather than a collection of disconnected exchanges. The focus then shifts from what is said in individual moments to how consistently the system is applied over time. Which is what the next chapter is about.

# CHAPTER 8
# MAKING IT REPEATABLE

A pipeline can be clearly defined. The stages can make sense. The movement can be logical. The messaging can be aligned. And still the results can vary. This is the point where many businesses begin to feel stuck, because the structure is present, the understanding is there and yet the outcomes remain inconsistent.

The reason for this is almost never a flaw in the design of the pipeline itself. It is a lack of consistency in how it is applied. A pipeline is not valuable because it exists. It is valuable because it is used in a reliable way over time. That sounds simple. In practice, it is where most systems begin to quietly weaken.

Consistency is not created by intention. It is created by behaviour that occurs repeatedly under normal working conditions, not the ideal conditions of a quiet morning when focus is easy, but the ordinary ones where the inbox is full and three other things need attention simultaneously. That behaviour is shaped by habits, and those habits are shaped by how the work itself is structured. When a pipeline depends on memory, motivation or the availability of spare time, it cannot be relied upon to produce stable outcomes. And those three things are always in shorter supply than anyone expects.

The way this plays out is rarely dramatic. It does not begin with a decision to stop applying the process. It begins with small, entirely reasonable adjustments that accumulate over time into something that looks very different from where it started.

A follow-up is delayed by a day. A conversation is left until later because something else felt more urgent. A next step is assumed rather than clearly stated because the interaction seemed to be going well enough without it. None of these moments appear significant on their own. Over time, they become the reason movement begins to vary in ways that are difficult to explain.

In the first week, the difference may not be obvious at all. New enquiries are still being answered. Some conversations are still moving. Follow-ups are still being completed often enough that the pipeline appears active. At this stage, the process feels intact. If something is missed, it feels incidental rather than structural.

By the fourth week, a different pattern begins to emerge. Some conversations are being progressed consistently while others are handled only when they happen to return to attention. Follow-ups that should happen within a clear timeframe are being postponed. Enquiries remain in the same stage for longer than expected. Nothing has failed in a visible or dramatic way, but the rhythm has become uneven. The system is still present, but it is no longer being applied with the same level of attention it received at the beginning.

By the third month, the effect is easier to recognise but harder to reverse. The pipeline has not disappeared, but its reliability has weakened. Some parts are still functioning well, usually where the interaction is recent or the prospect is highly engaged. Other parts have begun to drift. Older conversations sit unresolved. Follow-ups are irregular. Next steps are not always introduced clearly. Movement still occurs, but it is no longer consistent enough to produce stable outcomes across the full volume of enquiry activity.

This is what system decay looks like in practice. It does not begin with collapse. It begins with small departures from the process that gradually become normal. A stage is skipped because the situation feels straightforward enough not to need it. A follow-up is delayed because something else feels more urgent. A conversation is handled from instinct rather than from structure because it seems easier in the moment. Each individual decision is understandable. Together, they weaken the system in a way that is cumulative and quiet.

When this happens repeatedly, the pipeline begins to rely more on judgement than on process. Strong conversations still move forward. Easy decisions still convert. Recent enquiries still receive attention. What gets lost is everything the pipeline was designed to catch, the follow-ups that are not urgent, the conversations that paused without drama, the interactions that need revisiting rather than reacting to. Conversations that need revisiting begin to lose visibility. Interactions that pause at an uncertain point are less likely to be resumed. The pipeline shifts from being a working system to being a loose framework that is applied selectively, to the conversations that are already performing well rather than the ones that need structure to move at all.

This change is often missed because the business continues to operate in a way that looks normal from the outside. Messages are still sent. Responses are still received. Some outcomes are still achieved. What becomes less visible is the growing number of interactions that are not being carried through to a defined outcome. The business appears active. The underlying flow is something else.

This is why repeatability matters more than structure alone. A well-designed pipeline that is not maintained consistently will gradually lose its effect. The stages may still exist. The messaging may still make sense. The process may still be understood conceptually. But if it is not applied in the same way across time, the output begins to vary and that variation tends to compound rather than correct itself.

The underlying issue is not usually capability. Most businesses are perfectly able to handle enquiries well in individual moments. The problem is that strong individual moments do not automatically produce a repeatable system. A single well-managed conversation does not compensate for multiple conversations that are left incomplete. Consistency is what connects those individual moments into an overall result that is stable.

This is where rhythm becomes important. Certain actions need to occur regularly if the pipeline is to remain active and useful. New enquiries need to be responded to within a clear timeframe. Conversations in progress need to be reviewed consistently. Follow-ups need to happen when they should, not when they happen to be remembered. Decision-stage enquiries need to remain visible until a conclusion is actually reached. When these actions have a defined place in the structure of a working day or week, the process becomes less dependent on memory and mood. The system begins to hold its shape under normal working conditions rather than only when given special attention.

When that rhythm is missing, the opposite happens. Work becomes reactive. Recent enquiries receive attention because they are visible and immediate. Older conversations receive less attention because they require deliberate re-entry. Follow-ups become irregular because they are not triggered by anything in the system. They rely on recollection, which is an unreliable foundation. Decisions that should be supported by continuity are left to chance. Over time, this does not only reduce movement. It changes the nature of the pipeline. It becomes something that records activity rather than something that actively guides it.

A useful way to understand this is to look at the pipeline at different points in time. In week one, it may still feel manageable through attention alone. By week four, the accumulation of unresolved interactions begins to create friction that requires increasing effort to address. By month three, the effect is large enough to alter outcomes in a measurable way. The same business may still be generating the same number of enquiries, but the proportion that reaches a decision becomes less stable because the process is no longer being applied with the same consistency it had at the beginning.

This is also where abandonment tends to happen and it is worth being honest about this because it is more common than most people like to admit. A pipeline is rarely abandoned through a deliberate decision. More often, it is used less and less until it no longer shapes behaviour in any meaningful way. The stages remain visible in a CRM, a spreadsheet or an inbox process, but they are no longer influencing what happens next. Updates become occasional. Follow-up depends on recollection. The structure is still technically there, but it is no longer active.

When a system reaches this point, it usually produces two misleading impressions simultaneously. First, it still appears organised because the framework exists and can be pointed to. Second, it still produces some results because certain conversations continue to convert regardless of structural support. These impressions make the decay harder to identify. The business may conclude that the pipeline is working well enough when in reality it is only functioning partially. The cost of this is not usually visible in the completed interactions. It appears in the growing number of conversations that never reach a conclusion and are never recorded as anything because they did not fail loudly enough to be noticed.

What abandonment looks like in practice is not dramatic. An enquiry is answered and then left open without a clear next step. A consultation is discussed but not booked because the conversation felt good enough to leave there. A booked conversation is not followed through after the appointment. A paused interaction remains untouched for weeks because nothing in the system brings it back into view. No single moment appears decisive. The pattern is cumulative. The pipeline is no longer producing movement consistently. It is simply hosting activity.

To prevent this, repeatability has to be built into the normal flow of work rather than treated as an additional task to be completed when time allows. This does not require complexity. In fact, complexity often makes consistency harder to maintain rather than easier, because it creates more decisions and more friction at the point where the habit is meant to form. What is needed is a routine that makes the next action visible and expected. New enquiries are checked at defined intervals. Ongoing conversations are reviewed regularly. Stalled interactions are revisited. Decision-stage enquiries remain active until a conclusion is reached. The specifics will vary between businesses, but the principle remains the same. Regular attention produces movement. Irregular attention produces stagnation.

Visibility is part of this. A pipeline that is difficult to access, difficult to interpret or difficult to update is unlikely to be used consistently regardless of how well it is designed. It becomes something that exists in theory rather than in practice, something you intend to use rather than something you actually use. A usable pipeline is one that can be reviewed quickly and understood without significant effort. The current stage of each enquiry is clear. The next action is visible. When this is true, consistent use becomes far more likely. When it is not, the urgent always wins. The pipeline retreats until it exists in theory but not in practice.

This is why repeatability is not simply about discipline. It is about reducing the number of decisions required to keep the system active. The more the pipeline relies on remembering, interpreting and improvising, the less stable it becomes over time. The more it prompts action clearly and consistently, the more dependable the outcomes become, not because anything dramatic has changed, but because the small consistent actions that drive the system are happening reliably instead of occasionally.

Over longer periods, this difference compounds in ways that become difficult to ignore. A repeatable pipeline produces a steadier flow of movement through the stages. More conversations reach defined points. Fewer remain unresolved without explanation. Follow-up is not perfect in every case, but it is consistent enough that the structure continues to function under normal conditions. Without repeatability, even a strong design will under-perform, because the process loses force as it moves through the real conditions of a working business rather than the idealised conditions in which it was designed.

At that point the distinction becomes clear. A pipeline is not effective because it is well described. It is effective because it continues to operate when the initial clarity has faded, when work becomes busy and when multiple conversations need to be managed at once. If it can do that, it becomes part of how the business actually runs. If it cannot, it remains an idea that works only when given special attention. That is what repeatability determines. It is the difference between a process that makes sense and a process that continues to work.

# CHAPTER 9
# PIPELINES IN PRACTICE

## Jewellery Retail

A jewellery enquiry often begins with a clear intent, but not always a clear decision. The person making the enquiry may already have something specific in mind or they may still be exploring options. In both cases, the conversation that follows determines whether that initial interest develops into a purchase. The example below follows a typical enquiry from first contact through to outcome, first without structure and then with a defined process applied.

Without Structure

An enquiry comes in through the website:
"Hi, I'm looking for an engagement ring. Around $5–7k. Do you have anything available?"

The message is seen later in the day and a response is sent:
"Hi, yes we do have a range in that price. Feel free to come in store or let me know what style you're after."

At this point, the interaction appears complete. The question has been answered and an option has been provided. From the perspective of the business, the conversation is open. From the perspective of the person making the enquiry, a small evaluation is taking place. The response is read, but it does not create a clear reason to continue. The path forward is implied rather than defined.

There is no immediate reply.

Later that day, other enquiries come in and the conversation moves down the inbox. It remains visible, but no longer recent. The following day, there is still no reply and the message is not revisited because there is no defined reason to return to it. After several days, the enquiry is no longer considered active. It has not been closed, but it is no longer part of the current workload.

Nothing in this exchange is incorrect. The response is polite and accurate and the enquiry has been acknowledged. What is missing is direction. The conversation does not establish a next step and leaves the responsibility with the customer to decide how to proceed. In many cases, this results in no further movement.

With Structure

The same enquiry comes in:
"Hi, I'm looking for an engagement ring. Around $5–7k. Do you have anything available?"

The response is sent within a similar timeframe, but the structure is different:
"Hi, yes, we have a number of options in that range. Are you looking for something classic or something more custom? I can send through a few options if that helps."

The conversation now has a direction.

The person reads the message. There is a brief pause. At this point, nothing has been decided, but a small evaluation is taking place. The response has answered the question and introduced a path forward. The question now is whether it feels easy to continue.

The customer replies later that day:
"Something classic. Solitaire style."

The next step is defined within the reply and the response continues the movement of the conversation:
"That's helpful. I'll send through three options in that style within your range. If one stands out, we can either hold it or arrange a time for you to see it in person."

Images are sent shortly after.

At this point, the conversation pauses and there is no reply that evening. This pause is often interpreted as disinterest. In practice, it is more often a point of consideration. The person may be comparing options, thinking about budget or discussing the decision with someone else. The conversation has not ended, but it has slowed.

The following day, the conversation is still active. It has not been completed, so a follow-up is sent:

"Just checking you received the options I sent through. Let me know if one is close or if you'd like to see something slightly different."

The follow-up does not restart the conversation. It continues it. It refers to what has already been discussed, which reduces the effort required to re-engage. Instead of beginning again, the interaction resumes from its previous position.

Later that day, the customer replies:
"I like the second one. Do you have it in white gold?"

The conversation continues:
"Yes, we do. I can have it ready for you to view. Are you planning to come in this week or next?"

The next step is made explicit within the exchange and the customer responds:
"Next week would be better."

A time is offered as part of the same progression:
"We have Thursday afternoon or Saturday morning available. Let me know what suits."

The appointment is confirmed.

Between the enquiry and the visit, the conversation remains active. If needed, a short confirmation message is sent: "Just confirming for Saturday. I'll have that piece ready for you." This maintains continuity and reduces the likelihood of the interaction fading before the next step is completed.

After the visit, the interaction does not immediately end. There is a period where the decision is still being processed. The person has seen the piece, but may still be considering the purchase. In some cases, this leads directly to a sale. In others, it leads to hesitation.

A brief follow-up at this stage reinforces continuity: "It was great to meet you on Saturday. Let me know if you'd like me to hold that piece for you or if you'd like to see any alternatives." This keeps the interaction open and moves it toward a defined decision point rather than allowing it to remain unresolved.

In some cases, the decision is not immediate. Several days may pass while the person considers price, compares options or waits for the right moment to commit. During this period, the conversation can easily become inactive if it is treated as complete simply because the visit has already taken place. With structure, that does not happen.

A few days later, the interaction can be revisited in a way that reflects what has already occurred:
"Just checking in on the ring you saw on Saturday. Happy to hold it for a few more days if that would help or to show you one or two similar options if you're still comparing." This does not restart the process. It continues it from the point it had already reached.

In some situations, the person may not reply for a week or more. Without structure, the interaction would usually end there. With structure, a later re-engagement is still possible because the context has been preserved. A message sent after a longer pause can refer directly to the earlier visit and keep the path open without pressure. This is often where a decision that appeared to have disappeared is brought back into motion.

### Where Movement Occurs

The difference between the two examples is not the enquiry, but the structure of the interaction over time. In the first case, the conversation is acknowledged but not directed. There is no defined next step and no continuation if the customer does not respond, so as new activity comes in the earlier enquiry becomes less visible.

In the second case, the conversation is carried forward deliberately. Each response introduces a next step and when the interaction slows it is revisited. The enquiry remains part of the active pipeline until it reaches a defined point.

This does not guarantee an outcome. The customer may still decide not to proceed. What changes is the likelihood that the conversation reaches a point where that decision is made.

### Where Conversations Stall

Even with structure, not every enquiry progresses immediately. In jewellery retail, conversations often slow at predictable points such as after initial options are sent, after a preference is expressed but not confirmed, between selecting an item and arranging a visit and after a visit while a decision is being considered.

Each of these points represents a different type of hesitation. After options are sent, the hesitation is often comparative. After a preference is expressed, it may relate to uncertainty about the final choice. After a visit, it often relates to commitment.

In each case, the conversation has not ended. It has paused at a point where a next step has not yet been taken. Without a defined process, these pauses often become endpoints. With structure, they become points of continuation.

Applying Consistency

The role of the pipeline is not to force movement, but to maintain it. Where a conversation slows, it is revisited in a way that relates to what has already been discussed, for example by checking in on a previously mentioned option or offering to show similar alternatives. These are not new conversations but continuations of existing ones.

Over time, this approach changes how enquiries behave. Fewer are left without a conclusion and more reach a clear outcome, whether that is a purchase or a decision not to proceed.

## Hair Clinic

A hair clinic enquiry often begins with uncertainty rather than a clear decision. The person reaching out is usually trying to understand what is happening and whether it can be addressed, rather than committing to a specific treatment. The conversation that follows determines whether that uncertainty is clarified and carried forward or left unresolved.

The example below follows a typical enquiry from first contact through to outcome, first without structure and then with a defined process applied.

Without Structure

An enquiry comes in through the website or social media:
"Hi, I've noticed my hair thinning over the last few months. Do you treat this?"

The message is seen and a response is sent:
"Hi, yes we do treat hair thinning. It depends on the cause. You can book a consultation if you'd like."

At this point, the question has been answered, but a second layer of evaluation is taking place. The person is not only asking whether treatment exists. They are trying to understand what is happening and whether their situation is understood. The response provides information, but it does not reduce that uncertainty or create a clear path forward.

Over the first day, the enquiry sits in an early stage. The question has been answered, but the direction of the conversation is not yet established.

There is no immediate reply.

By the second day, the interaction begins to lose visibility. Other messages take priority and, without a defined reason to return to it, the conversation moves out of focus. Later that day, additional enquiries come in and the message moves further down the inbox. It remains visible, but no longer current.

The following day, there is still no reply and the message is not revisited because there is no defined reason to return to it. After several days, the enquiry is no longer considered active. It has not been resolved, but it is no longer part of the working set of conversations.

Nothing in this exchange is incorrect. The question has been answered and the option of a consultation has been mentioned. What is missing is direction. The response provides information, but it does not guide the conversation forward or reduce uncertainty in a way that makes the next step easier to take. As a result, the interaction remains open and, in many cases, does not progress further.

With Structure

The same enquiry comes in:
"Hi, I've noticed my hair thinning over the last few months. Do you treat this?"

The response is sent within a similar timeframe, but the structure is different:
"Hi, yes, we do treat hair thinning. Has this come on gradually or have you noticed it more recently? I can explain what we usually look at first if that helps."

The conversation now has a direction.

At this stage, the person is not evaluating a treatment. They are evaluating whether their situation is being understood. The question introduced here shifts the interaction from information to understanding, which reduces uncertainty and makes it easier to continue.

The person replies later that day:
"It's been gradual over maybe six months."

Within the same day, the conversation has moved beyond the initial question. Context has been introduced and the next step has begun to take shape. The next step is defined within the response, which continues the interaction:
"That helps. In cases like that, we usually start with a short consultation to understand the cause and talk through what can be done. I can explain how that works or we can look at a time for you to come in."

At this point, the conversation shifts. It is no longer about whether treatment exists. It is about whether the person is ready to take a step toward it.

This is where hesitation often increases. The idea of a consultation introduces commitment. The person is no longer gathering information. They are being asked to act. If the conversation stops here, it is not necessarily rejection. It is often uncertainty about what that step involves.

At this point, the interaction pauses and there is no reply that evening.

The following day, the enquiry remains active within the pipeline. It has not reached a conclusion, so a follow-up is sent that relates directly to what has already been discussed:

“Just checking if you wanted me to run through what we would cover in the consultation or if you’d prefer to look at a time to come in.”

The follow-up does not introduce pressure. It reduces uncertainty. It clarifies what happens next rather than pushing for a decision.

Later that day, the person replies:
“Yes, can you explain what happens in the consultation?”

The conversation continues with more detail:
“We would look at your scalp and hair pattern, talk through what you’ve noticed and outline what options are appropriate based on that. From there, you can decide what you’d like to do next.”

This makes the process more visible and reduces hesitation.

At this point, typically within a few days of the initial enquiry, the conversation has progressed to a defined next step. The next step is then introduced more clearly within the same flow:
“If you’d like, I can book that in for you this week or next.”

The person responds:
“Next week would be better.”

A time is offered as part of the progression:
“We have Tuesday morning or Thursday afternoon available. Let me know what suits.”

The appointment is confirmed.

Between the initial enquiry and the consultation, the conversation remains active. A short confirmation message closer to the time maintains continuity and reduces the likelihood of the interaction fading before the appointment.

Between booking and attending, there is a second layer of hesitation. The decision has been made in principle, but not yet completed in action. Without continuity, this can result in delays or cancellations.

After the consultation, the interaction may pause again. This is a different type of hesitation. The person now has more information, but may need time to decide whether to proceed. Without a structured follow-up, this often becomes an unresolved interaction.

With structure, the conversation is revisited:
"Just checking how you're feeling after the consultation. Let me know if you'd like to go ahead or if you have any questions." This moves the interaction toward a defined decision point rather than leaving it open.

In some cases, the decision still takes time. Days or weeks may pass before the person is ready to act. Without structure, the conversation would usually end during this period. With structure, a later re-engagement is still possible because the interaction has been maintained rather than abandoned.

A follow-up after a longer pause can refer back to the consultation and keep the path open without pressure. This is often where decisions that appeared to have stalled begin to move again.

## Where Movement Occurs

The difference between the two examples is not the enquiry, but how uncertainty is handled over time. In the first case, the question is answered, but the conversation is not guided. There is no clear next step and no continuation if the person does not respond, so the interaction becomes inactive as new messages take priority.

In the second case, the conversation is carried forward deliberately. Each response introduces a next step and, when the interaction slows, it is revisited in a way that reflects what has already been discussed. The enquiry remains part of the active pipeline until it reaches a defined point.

This does not guarantee that the person will proceed with treatment. What changes is the likelihood that the conversation reaches a point where a decision is made, rather than remaining unresolved.

## Where Conversations Stall

Even with structure, not every enquiry progresses immediately. In a hair clinic setting, conversations often slow at points where uncertainty is highest, such as after an initial explanation is given, when the idea of a consultation is introduced, during the period between booking and attending and after the consultation while a decision is being considered.

Each of these points reflects a different type of hesitation. Early hesitation relates to understanding. Mid-stage hesitation relates to commitment. Later hesitation relates to decision-making.

In each case, the conversation has not ended. It has paused at a point where more clarity is needed before a next step is taken. Without a defined process, these pauses often become endpoints. With structure, they become points of continuation.

Applying Consistency

The role of the pipeline is not to remove uncertainty, but to carry the conversation through it. Where an interaction slows, it is revisited in a way that relates to what has already been discussed, whether by offering further explanation or clarifying the next step. These are not new conversations but continuations of existing ones.

Over time, this approach changes how enquiries behave. More reach a point where a decision is made and fewer remain open without a clear outcome.

**Med Spa**

A med spa enquiry tends to arrive somewhere between curiosity and intent. The person reaching out is usually aware of the treatment they are considering. They are not quite browsing and not quite decided. They want to know whether it is right for them specifically, whether the outcome will be what they are hoping for and whether the treatment feels manageable. The question they send is often about price or availability. The evaluation they are actually making is considerably more personal than that.

Without Structure

An enquiry comes in through the website or social media.

"Hi, I'm interested in lip filler. How much does it cost?"

The message is seen and a response is sent.

"Hi, lip filler starts from $X. Feel free to book a consultation."

At this point the question has technically been answered. But the evaluation taking place on the other end is about more than price.

The person is asking whether this is the right place, whether the result will look natural, whether they will feel comfortable with the process. The response provides a number and a direction, but it does not address any of that underlying uncertainty.

There is no immediate reply.

By the second day the interaction begins to lose visibility. Other enquiries arrive and, without a defined reason to revisit the conversation, it moves out of focus. After several days the enquiry is no longer considered active. The price was given. The consultation was mentioned. Nothing came of it.

Nothing in this exchange is incorrect. But it treats the question at face value when the real question sits one layer underneath. As a result, the interaction remains open and in most cases does not progress.

With Structure

The same enquiry comes in.

"Hi, I'm interested in lip filler. How much does it cost?"

The response is sent within a similar timeframe, but the structure is different.

"Hi, the cost depends a little on the look you're going for. Are you after something subtle and natural, or more definition and volume?"

The conversation now has a direction.

This question does something specific. It shifts the interaction from price to outcome, which is where the person's actual evaluation is already happening. It also signals that the response on the other end is coming from someone who understands the treatment, not just someone who knows the price list.

The person replies.

"Something natural. I just want a bit more volume without it looking obvious."

The conversation has moved meaningfully. Context has been established. The person has shared something slightly vulnerable, which means trust is beginning to form.

"That's the most common thing people are looking for. For that kind of result, the consultation is actually the most useful step because it lets us look at the shape of your lips and talk through exactly what would work for you. A lot of people find it reassuring before they commit to anything."

The response continues the interaction and introduces the consultation in a way that reduces rather than adds pressure. It normalises the consultation as a useful step rather than presenting it as a gate that must be passed before anything else can happen.

The person replies.

"That sounds good. How does the consultation work?"

The follow-up explains the process clearly.

"It's a short appointment where we look at your lips, talk through what you're hoping for and go through what the treatment involves. There's no obligation to book anything after. It just gives you a much clearer picture of what's possible."

This removes the commitment that often sits as an unspoken barrier between interest and action. The person is not being asked to decide. They are being invited to understand.

At this point the conversation moves toward booking.

"If you'd like to come in, I can look at times for you. Are you generally more available during the week or at weekends?"

The person responds. "Weekends are easier."

A time is offered. "We have Saturday late morning available next week. Would that suit?"

The appointment is confirmed.

Between the enquiry and the consultation, the conversation remains active. A brief confirmation closer to the appointment maintains continuity and reduces the likelihood that the interaction fades in the days before it.

After the consultation, a follow-up keeps the path open without pressure.

"It was great to meet you. Let me know if you'd like to go ahead or if you have any other questions. I'm happy to answer anything."

In cases where the decision takes longer, the interaction can be revisited.

"Just checking in. No pressure at all, but let me know if you'd like to book in when you're ready."

This keeps the door open without implying impatience. The person knows the option is still available without feeling chased.

## Where Movement Occurs

The difference between the two examples is not the enquiry. It is how the underlying evaluation is handled. In the first case the question is answered at face value and the conversation is not guided beyond that point. In the second case the response engages with what the person is actually trying to figure out, which creates a different kind of interaction from the beginning.

That difference compounds as the conversation progresses. Each response in the structured version does something specific. It acknowledges what has been said, introduces context and moves the interaction toward the next step. When the conversation slows, it is revisited in a way that maintains the connection rather than restarting it from the beginning.

## Where Conversations Stall

In a med spa setting, hesitation tends to cluster around three points. After the initial price or availability question is answered. When the consultation is introduced. And after the consultation while a decision is being considered.

The first type of hesitation is often about fit. The person is not sure this is the right place or the right time or the right treatment for them. The second type is about commitment. Moving from asking to doing requires a step that many people pause at, particularly when the treatment involves their appearance. The third type is about certainty. Even after a consultation, the decision to proceed can sit with someone for longer than expected.

In each case, the conversation has not ended. It has paused. Without a defined process, those pauses tend to become permanent. With structure they become something the pipeline accounts for rather than something it mistakes for a decision.

Applying Consistency

The role of the pipeline here is to remain present without being intrusive. The person making this kind of enquiry is often managing a private consideration, something they have been thinking about for a while but have not discussed openly with many people. The pipeline that handles this well is one that keeps the conversation available without pushing it, that follows up in a way that feels like genuine interest rather than a sales process.

Over time this changes the proportion of enquiries that reach a conclusion. Not all of them will. But more will reach the point where the person has genuinely decided, one way or the other, rather than simply drifting away while the question was still open.

### Cosmetic Dental Clinic

A cosmetic dental enquiry often begins with intent, but also with hesitation. The person reaching out is usually aware of the treatment they are considering, but the decision carries more weight. Cost, time, perceived risk and outcome all play a role. The conversation that follows determines whether that initial intent develops into a committed step forward or remains under consideration.

The example below follows a typical enquiry from first contact through to outcome, first without structure and then with a defined process applied.

Without Structure

An enquiry comes in through the website:
"Hi, I'm interested in veneers. Can you tell me how much they cost?"

The message is seen and a response is sent:
"Hi, veneers vary depending on the case. It's best to come in for a

consultation."

At this point, the question has been answered, but a second layer of evaluation is taking place. The person is not only asking about price. They are trying to understand what is involved, what result might be possible and whether the treatment feels realistic for them. The response points toward consultation, but it does not reduce that uncertainty or create a clear path forward.

Over the first day, the enquiry sits in an early stage. The question has been answered, but the direction of the conversation is not yet established.

There is no immediate reply.

By the second day, the interaction begins to lose visibility. Other enquiries take priority and, without a defined reason to return to it, the conversation moves out of focus. Later that day, additional enquiries come in and the message moves down the inbox. It remains visible, but no longer current.

The following day, there is still no reply and the message is not revisited because there is no defined reason to return to it. After several days, the enquiry is no longer considered active. It has not been closed, but it is no longer part of the working set of conversations.

Nothing in this exchange is incorrect. The response is accurate and it points toward the appropriate next step. What is missing is context and progression. The conversation moves quickly to consultation without first establishing what the person is trying to achieve and it does not reduce the uncertainty that often sits behind the initial question. As a result, the interaction remains open and, in many cases, does not progress further.

With Structure

The same enquiry comes in:
"Hi, I'm interested in veneers. Can you tell me how much they cost?"

The response is sent within a similar timeframe, but the structure is different:
"Hi, veneers can vary quite a bit depending on what you're looking to

change. Are you mainly looking at colour, shape or a full smile transformation?"

The conversation now has a direction.

At this stage, the person is not simply evaluating cost. They are evaluating whether the treatment matches what they want to achieve. The question introduced here shifts the interaction from price to outcome. That change is small, but it alters the direction of the conversation.

The person replies later that day:
"Mostly colour and a bit of shape."

Within the same day, the conversation has moved beyond the initial question. Context has been introduced, but hesitation remains. The person has indicated intent, but has not yet committed to a next step.

The next step is defined within the response, which continues the interaction:
"That helps. In cases like that, we usually start with a consultation where we look at your current smile, talk through what you'd like to achieve and map out what's possible. I can give you a clearer idea of pricing after that, but I can also outline a general range if that's useful."

The person replies:
"Yes, a range would help."

The response continues:
"For what you've described, it typically falls within a certain range depending on the number of teeth involved. We can go through that in more detail at consultation, but that gives you a starting point."

At this point, the conversation pauses and there is no reply that evening. This is often where hesitation becomes more pronounced. The person now has enough information to understand that the treatment is possible, but not yet enough certainty to decide. The question is no longer whether veneers are available. It is whether the treatment feels appropriate, achievable and worth taking further.

The following day, the enquiry remains active within the pipeline. It

has not reached a conclusion, so a follow-up is sent that relates to what has already been discussed:
"Just checking if you wanted to look at what the consultation involves or if you'd prefer to find a time that suits."

The follow-up continues the interaction. It makes the next step easier to consider without increasing pressure.

Later that day, the person replies:
"What happens in the consultation?"

The conversation continues with more detail:
"We would assess your current teeth, talk through the changes you're looking for and show you what that could look like. From there, we can outline a plan and you can decide how you'd like to proceed."

This reduces uncertainty and makes the process more tangible.

At this point, typically within a few days of the initial enquiry, the conversation has progressed to a defined next step. The next step is then introduced more clearly within the same flow:
"If you'd like, I can book that in for you this week or next."

The person responds:
"Next week would be better."

A time is offered as part of the progression:
"We have Monday afternoon or Wednesday morning available. Let me know what works."

The appointment is confirmed.

Between the enquiry and the consultation, the conversation remains active. A short confirmation message may be sent closer to the time to maintain continuity. This reduces the likelihood that the interaction fades between commitment and attendance.

Between booking and attending, there is another layer of hesitation. The decision has been made in principle, but not yet completed in action. In higher-value treatments, this gap matters. Without continuity, the conversation can weaken even after a consultation has been booked.

After the consultation, the interaction may pause again. This is often the most significant point of hesitation. The person now has a clearer understanding of what is involved, but the decision requires consideration of cost, timing and outcome. Without a structured follow-up, this often becomes an unresolved interaction.

With structure, the conversation is revisited:
"Just checking how you're feeling after the consultation. Let me know if you'd like to go ahead or if you'd like to talk through anything again."

This does not push for a decision before the person is ready. It keeps the path open and moves the interaction toward a defined outcome.

In some cases, the decision takes longer. Days or weeks may pass while the person considers the treatment. Without structure, the conversation would usually end during this period. With structure, the interaction can be revisited in a way that reflects what has already been discussed. This is often where decisions that appeared to have stalled begin to move again.

### Where Movement Occurs

The difference between the two examples is not the enquiry, but how hesitation is handled over time. In the first case, the conversation moves quickly to consultation without building context and, when the person does not respond, the interaction is not revisited.

In the second case, the conversation is carried forward deliberately. Each response reduces uncertainty and introduces a next step and, when the interaction slows, it is revisited in a way that reflects what has already been discussed. The enquiry remains part of the active pipeline until it reaches a defined point.

This does not guarantee that the person will proceed with treatment. In higher-value decisions, that outcome may take longer. What changes is the likelihood that the conversation reaches a point where a decision is made, rather than remaining unresolved.

### Where Conversations Stall

Even with structure, not every enquiry progresses immediately. In a cosmetic dental setting, conversations often slow at predictable points. This commonly occurs after an initial price range is mentioned, when the consultation is introduced, during the period between booking and attending or after the consultation while a decision is being considered.

At each of these points, the decision becomes more concrete. Cost, timing and perceived outcome come into focus. Early hesitation relates to uncertainty about suitability. Mid-stage hesitation relates to commitment. Later hesitation relates to whether the treatment should go ahead.

The conversation does not end, but it pauses while these factors are weighed. Without a defined process, these pauses often become endpoints. The absence of a reply is treated as a decision and the interaction is not revisited.

With structure, these moments are treated differently. A pause is not assumed to be final. The conversation is revisited in a way that reflects what has already been discussed, whether by clarifying an aspect of the treatment, restating the plan or making the next step easier to take.

Over time, this changes how enquiries behave. More reach a point where a decision is made, even if that decision takes a while to arrive.

Applying Consistency

The role of the pipeline is not to accelerate decisions, but to maintain continuity through them. Where an interaction slows, it is revisited in a way that relates to what has already been discussed. These are not new conversations but continuations of existing ones.

Over time, this approach changes how enquiries behave. More reach a point where a decision is made and fewer remain open without a clear outcome.

Across all four examples, the structure remains consistent even though the enquiries themselves differ.

In jewellery, the conversation moves from selection toward purchase.

In a hair clinic, it moves from uncertainty toward understanding and consultation.

In a med spa setting, it moves from interest toward suitability and outcome.

In cosmetic dental, it moves from intent toward a considered decision.

The sequence changes in detail, but not in principle.

Each enquiry begins with a question. Each develops through stages. Each reaches points where it slows. Each requires a next step to continue. Without structure, those steps are inconsistent. With structure, they become deliberate.

The difference is not in the volume of enquiries or the type of business. It is in how the conversation is carried from one stage to the next and how consistently that movement is maintained over time. This is where the pipeline shifts from being a concept to something observable. It is no longer theoretical. It can be seen in how conversations behave, where they pause and how they continue.

Once that is visible, the next question is not how the pipeline is designed or how conversations should move in theory. It is how consistently that movement is applied in practice across all enquiries, not just the ones that are easiest to manage. That is what determines whether the system holds. And that is where most pipelines begin to weaken.

The stages define where a conversation sits. The messaging determines how it moves. The structure shows what should happen. What remains is whether it happens consistently enough for the pipeline to function as a system rather than a series of individual interactions. That is what we look at next.

# CHAPTER 10
# WHERE THIS BREAKS DOWN

Understanding how a pipeline works is one thing. Understanding why it stops working is another and altogether more useful skill.

In most cases the breakdown does not happen in a single moment. There is no obvious failure, no conversation that collapses dramatically and no decision that can be pointed to as the turning point. It develops gradually, through a series of small decisions that each seem reasonable at the time. A message is answered but not directed. A conversation pauses and is not revisited. A follow-up is delayed because something more immediate needs attention. Each of these actions appears minor when viewed in isolation. There is no clear indication that anything has gone wrong and no immediate consequence that draws attention to the change.

The effect only becomes visible when those decisions are viewed across time.

In the first week, a small number of conversations remain incomplete. They are still recent and still visible, which creates the sense that they can be picked up again without difficulty. There is no urgency because nothing appears to have been lost. The interactions have not ended in any formal sense and they do not yet feel inactive. They simply sit in the background while more immediate tasks take priority, close enough to the surface that they still feel recoverable at any moment.

By the second week, those same conversations are no longer current. New enquiries have entered the system and moved into focus and the earlier interactions begin to lose visibility. The intention to return to them may still exist, but it becomes less immediate as attention shifts toward what is recent. The effort required to re-engage has increased slightly because the context of the original conversation is no longer fresh. At this stage the conversations have not been closed. They have simply, quietly, moved out of the active pipeline.

By the third week the distinction becomes more pronounced. The conversations that were once active have now become dormant.

They have not reached a decision and they have not been resolved. They have simply stopped moving. At this point they are rarely revisited, not because they are deliberately ignored but because they no longer present themselves as immediate tasks. The pipeline continues to operate, but these interactions are no longer part of its visible movement. They sit outside of attention even though they were once fully inside it.

Over the course of a month this pattern repeats. New enquiries arrive. Some progress and others pause. The paused conversations accumulate gradually. Each one represents an interaction that could have continued but did not. Because the accumulation happens over time rather than in a single instance, it is difficult to recognise as a pattern. There is no single moment where a significant loss is observed. Instead, small amounts of value are lost repeatedly and quietly, in ways that feel like normal variation rather than structural failure.

This accumulation is what makes the breakdown so difficult to see clearly. An enquiry that could have progressed remains incomplete. A conversation that could have continued becomes inactive. A decision that could have been reached is never made. None of these outcomes are recorded as failures. They are simply absent. And because they are not recorded, they are not measured. And because they are not measured, they are not addressed. The absence does not register in the same way a clear loss would.

From the outside, the business continues to operate in a way that appears entirely normal. Enquiries are coming in. Responses are being sent. Some conversions are happening. There is no obvious disruption to the flow of activity. The visible movement creates the impression that the system is functioning as expected. What is not visible is the volume of interactions that did not reach a conclusion and the cumulative effect that has over time. The activity that can be seen masks the activity that has quietly stopped.

As this pattern extends beyond the first month, the effect begins to compound. By the second and third month the number of unresolved interactions is no longer small. It becomes a meaningful portion of total enquiry activity. These are not new enquiries that failed immediately. They are existing enquiries that were once active and have gradually fallen out of the process. Because they are no longer visible in the day-to-day flow, they are not perceived as part of the current workload, even though they still represent unrealised outcomes. They exist outside attention but still within potential.

Over a period of three to six months this invisible loss becomes significant. The business may have handled hundreds of enquiries during that time. A percentage will have converted. Another percentage will have been clearly unsuitable from the beginning. What remains is a substantial group of interactions that did not reach a defined outcome, not because they were not viable, but because they were not carried through to completion. This is where the gap between potential and actual performance begins to widen in a way that is difficult to attribute to a single cause. The loss is spread across time rather than concentrated in one visible place.

At this stage the problem is rarely diagnosed correctly and what happens next is worth examining because it is almost universal.

The most visible metric in most businesses is the number of new enquiries coming in. When outcomes feel inconsistent, the instinctive response is to look at volume. If revenue is not where it should be, the assumption is often that more enquiries are needed to compensate. This leads to a focus on marketing, lead generation or increasing visibility. The response is directed toward what is easiest to measure and easiest to act on.

This feels logical because it is based on what can be seen. More enquiries should produce more outcomes. When that does not happen consistently, the assumption is that the volume is insufficient. What is not immediately visible is the proportion of existing enquiries that are not being carried through to a decision. The issue is not always the number of new opportunities entering the pipeline. It is the number of existing opportunities that are not reaching completion. The problem sits inside the pipeline rather than before it.

This creates a form of false positive. The business identifies that something is wrong, but the source of the problem is misinterpreted. Marketing appears to be the constraint because it is the most obvious lever. More effort is applied to generating new enquiries. In the short term, this can produce an increase in activity. The pipeline becomes fuller. There are more conversations taking place. For a brief period this can create the impression of improvement.

However, if the underlying structure has not changed, the same pattern just repeats at a higher volume. More enquiries enter the system and more of them fail to reach a conclusion. The absolute number of outcomes may increase, but the proportion remains unstable. The underlying gap is not closed. It is simply scaled. The inefficiency expands along with the activity, which is not the result anyone was hoping for.

This is why businesses can feel genuinely busy while still experiencing inconsistent results. Activity increases but progression does not improve at the same rate. The system is working harder but not more effectively. The additional effort is absorbed by the same structural limitations that were present before the extra marketing spend. The pressure increases without resolving the underlying issue.

Another reason this problem is so consistently misdiagnosed is that the loss is not concentrated in one place. It is distributed across many interactions, each of which appears minor on its own. The absence of a decision in one case does not seem significant. When this occurs across dozens or hundreds of interactions over several months, the cumulative effect becomes substantial. But because the loss is distributed, it is difficult to connect back to a single cause. There is no single point of failure to identify. There is just a general sense that the business is not quite producing what it should.

Without a defined structure, this pattern becomes embedded in how the business operates. Conversations are treated as complete when they are no longer active, rather than when a decision has actually been reached. The distinction between those two states is subtle but important. One represents a finished interaction. The other represents an incomplete interaction that has simply stopped moving. When that distinction is not made consistently, the pipeline begins to reflect activity rather than progression and the true state of the system becomes less clear than it appears.

Over time, this creates a widening gap between what the business is producing and what it could be producing from the same level of enquiry activity. That gap is not caused by a lack of demand. It is caused by the way that demand is handled once it arrives. The enquiries are present. They are simply not being carried through to a defined outcome in a consistent enough way.

The longer this pattern continues, the more it begins to feel normal. Some enquiries convert and others do not. Some conversations progress and others fade. Without a clear reference point, this variation appears natural rather than correctable. It does not immediately suggest that something is missing. It simply feels like part of how the business functions. The inconsistency becomes familiar, which is perhaps the most expensive thing that can happen to it, because familiar problems do not get fixed.

This is what makes the breakdown persistent. It does not trigger a clear response because it does not present itself as a single failure. It appears as variation, inconsistency or fluctuation, all of which are accepted as part of the operating environment rather than recognised as symptoms of a structural issue. The pattern hides inside what appears to be normal business behaviour.

Once the pattern is seen clearly, however, the interpretation changes. The missing outcomes are no longer abstract. They can be traced back to specific interactions that began, developed to a point and then stopped without reaching a conclusion. At that point the question begins to shift. It is no longer whether the business is generating enough enquiries. It becomes whether the enquiries that already exist are being carried through to a defined outcome.

That is where the breakdown occurs. And that is also, reassuringly, where the fix begins.

# CHAPTER 11
# WHAT THIS REPRESENTS

Up to this point the focus has been on process. How enquiries move, where they stall, what causes them to progress and how consistency affects outcomes over time. Each part has been examined so that the mechanics of the pipeline can be understood clearly. Taken together, however, these elements represent something broader than process alone. They describe a shift in how a business understands its own activity and, more importantly, how it understands the relationship between activity and revenue.

In many businesses, enquiry activity is treated as something that sits before revenue rather than as part of it. An enquiry is seen as potential, but not as something that already carries measurable value. The focus is placed on what has converted rather than on what is currently in motion. As a result, a large portion of commercial activity sits outside the way the business evaluates its own performance. It is acknowledged in practice but not measured in a structured way and because it is not measured it is rarely managed with the same level of attention that conversions receive.

What the pipeline makes visible is that this activity is not separate from revenue. It is the early stage of it. Each enquiry represents a point at which revenue could be created. This is not theoretical or speculative. A certain volume of enquiries, handled in a consistent way, will produce a predictable range of outcomes. When that consistency is not present the outcomes vary. The difference between those two states is what has been explored throughout this book, not as an abstract idea but as something that can be observed directly in how conversations behave over time.

Seen in this way, the pipeline is not simply a tool for managing conversations. It is a mechanism for converting existing activity into realised revenue. The structure does not create demand. It determines what happens to the demand that already exists. This distinction matters because it changes where attention is directed within the business. The pipeline moves from being seen as a support function to being recognised as part of the commercial core of the business itself, something that directly influences results rather than simply sitting alongside them.

This is where the perspective begins to widen in a way that is worth sitting with for a moment.

A pipeline is not only a sequence of stages and it is not only a method for organising enquiries. At a broader level it functions as an operating system. It determines how demand is received, how it is processed and how it is carried through to an outcome. In a reactive business, that operating system is informal. Conversations are handled in the moment. Attention follows what is visible. Decisions about what happens next are made on the fly and often inconsistently. Some interactions move forward because they receive the right attention at the right time. Others do not, even when the underlying opportunity is similar or better.

In a structured business the same activity is handled differently. The path is clearer. The stages are visible. The next step is more consistently defined. Conversations do not depend as heavily on memory, timing or instinct alone. This does not remove judgement from the process, but it changes the conditions under which judgement is used. Instead of compensating for the absence of structure, judgement operates within structure. That is a very different position and over time it produces very different outcomes.

Without this perspective, growth tends to be approached by increasing the volume of new enquiries. More leads are generated, more traffic is driven and more activity enters the system. In some cases this produces an increase in revenue. In others it produces a larger volume of partially completed interactions. When the underlying process is inconsistent, increasing the volume of enquiries does not resolve the issue. It expands it. More activity enters the pipeline but the same patterns of delay, omission and inconsistency remain. The gap between potential and actual revenue becomes larger rather than smaller, which is not the intended outcome of a marketing spend.

With a defined and repeatable structure the relationship changes. The same level of enquiry activity begins to produce more consistent outcomes. Conversations are carried forward rather than left incomplete. Decisions are reached more reliably. The variability that previously existed is reduced. At that point, growth is no longer dependent on increasing input alone. It becomes a function of how effectively existing activity is converted and how consistently that conversion process is applied across the full volume of enquiries.

This does not remove the need for new enquiries. It places them in context. They become one part of a system rather than the primary driver of results. The performance of the system itself becomes equally important. Over time this leads to a different understanding of where value is created within the business and how that value accumulates across multiple interactions rather than appearing only at the point of sale.

Value is not only generated at the point of conversion. It is generated throughout the interaction. Each stage of the pipeline contributes to whether an enquiry progresses or stalls. Each decision to follow up or not follow up, to guide or not guide, to continue or not continue has a cumulative effect on the outcome. When this is recognised, the absence of outcomes is no longer neutral. It is not simply the absence of a sale. It is the result of a process that did not carry the interaction to a conclusion, even though it could have.

This is why the pipeline should not be understood as an administrative layer sitting around the edges of revenue. It is not a matter of tidiness or organisation or communication style. It is a form of revenue control. It determines whether existing demand is being translated into outcomes with consistency or whether that demand is being lost through variation in how it is handled. Once seen in this way, the distinction between operational process and commercial performance begins to collapse. They are not separate. They are expressions of the same system viewed from different angles.

This reframes the idea of unrealised revenue. It is not something external to the business and it is not a missed opportunity in an abstract sense. It is the measurable difference between what existing enquiry activity is capable of producing and what it currently produces under inconsistent conditions. Once that difference is understood it becomes a reference point, a way to evaluate performance that goes beyond what has already happened.

Performance is no longer evaluated solely by what has been achieved. It is evaluated in relation to what could reasonably be achieved from the same level of activity. A period of strong revenue can be assessed against its potential. A period of weaker performance can be understood in terms of where the process has not functioned as intended. This does not remove variation. It makes it interpretable and, more importantly, it makes it actionable. There is a significant difference between knowing that something is wrong and being able to locate where it is happening.

The role of the pipeline is therefore not only operational. It is analytical. It provides a way to observe how enquiry activity behaves over time and how that behaviour translates into outcomes. It allows the business to see not only what is happening, but what should be happening under consistent conditions. That visibility changes how decisions are made. It shifts attention toward what influences outcomes rather than what merely records them.

Attention can be directed toward the points where movement slows. Adjustments can be made to how conversations are carried forward. The relationship between activity and outcome becomes clearer and more predictable. At that point the pipeline is no longer simply a structure applied to communication. It becomes a framework through which the business understands its own performance and a mechanism through which that performance can be influenced deliberately rather than hoped for.

This is what the preceding chapters lead to. Not a set of techniques, but a shift in perspective. The movement from viewing enquiries as isolated interactions to understanding them as part of a continuous process that produces measurable outcomes. It is also a shift in business identity. A reactive business responds to demand as it appears. A structured business manages demand as a system. One depends on attention in the moment. The other builds consistency into the movement itself and allows that consistency to compound over time.

Once that shift occurs, the question is no longer how to generate more activity. It becomes how to ensure that the activity that already exists is carried through to a defined outcome in a consistent way.

By this point the pattern should be clear. Revenue is not produced in a single moment. It is not the result of one conversation, one message or one decision. It is the result of a sequence that unfolds over time and that sequence behaves differently depending on how it is handled.

That sequence already exists inside the business. Enquiries come in, responses are sent and conversations begin. Some move forward, some pause and some disappear. Without structure that movement is inconsistent. With structure it becomes more reliable. This is the difference between activity and output and it is a difference that becomes more visible when viewed across multiple interactions rather than in isolation.

Most businesses do not lack effort. They lack a system that converts that effort into consistent movement. That is what creates the gap between what the business could produce and what it actually does. When that system is not defined, outcomes vary not because the individual handling the interaction is inconsistent, but because the process itself is. One conversation is handled well while another is not. A follow-up is applied at the right time in one case and missed in another. Over time these variations accumulate and they show up in the numbers, not as a single error but as a pattern of uneven results that is difficult to explain from inside the business.

With structure the same level of effort produces a different result. Conversations move with more clarity. Next steps are defined. Fewer enquiries stall without explanation. More reach a point where a decision can be made. This does not remove uncertainty, but it reduces unnecessary loss and makes the movement of the pipeline more predictable across the full volume of enquiry activity.

This is the shift. Revenue moves from being something that appears to depend on personal performance to something that emerges from a system. That system is not separate from the business. It is made up of the interactions that are already taking place. The enquiries that are received, the conversations that follow and the decisions that are reached over time. Nothing new needs to be created. What changes is how those elements are connected, how they move and how they are managed consistently under normal working conditions.

This is where most businesses stop. The idea is understood, the pattern is recognised and the gap is visible. Implementation, however, is left incomplete. Not because it lacks value, but because it requires more than a one-time adjustment. It requires ongoing attention, consistency and the ability to apply the structure across multiple conversations at different stages without allowing it to break down under the ordinary pressure of a busy working week.

This is where most systems fail. Not in design, but in application.

At this point there are two paths. The structure can be built and applied internally by defining stages, aligning messaging and establishing a rhythm that supports consistent movement across enquiries. This will produce improvement. Movement becomes more consistent, fewer interactions are left incomplete and the pipeline begins to behave in a more predictable way over time.

As this structure is introduced, a new requirement emerges. Consistency must be maintained across all interactions, not just those that happen to receive attention at the right moment. This applies across multiple conversations, at different stages and under varying levels of urgency. The process does not fail in a visible or dramatic way, but small lapses begin to accumulate. Follow-ups are missed. Next steps are not always introduced clearly. Momentum is lost in ways that are difficult to track in real time.

This is where most breakdown occurs. Not in understanding what needs to happen, but in applying it consistently across the full volume of enquiry activity and sustaining that consistency over time.

The alternative is to treat this not as a set of actions to be remembered and repeated, but as a system. Something that is designed and implemented so that it operates reliably without depending on constant manual attention. In this case the structure is not applied selectively. It is held in place across all enquiries, including those that would otherwise lose visibility over time or quietly fall out of the active pipeline.

The distinction is subtle but important. It marks the difference between knowing what to do and having it work in practice. One relies on ongoing effort to maintain consistency. The other embeds that consistency into the way the pipeline operates so that it continues to function under normal working conditions rather than only under focused attention.

At this stage the focus shifts from understanding to application. The question is no longer how enquiries should move in theory. It is how the current flow of enquiry activity aligns with that structure in practice. This can be observed directly by looking at how conversations are progressing, where they are pausing and which interactions are not reaching a defined outcome despite having developed far enough that they could have.

A simple review of existing enquiry activity provides a useful starting point. By examining how enquiries are currently moving through the pipeline and where structure is not being consistently applied, it becomes possible to identify where value is being lost and what changes would improve movement across the system as a whole.

From there the next step becomes clearer. The structure can be applied more deliberately, whether internally or through a system designed to maintain it consistently over time. The choice is not whether structure is needed. That question has been answered. The choice is how it is sustained and how soon.

Either way, the principle remains unchanged. Revenue is not a reflection of who you are. It is a reflection of how your process works. And that process is something that can be built, applied and improved with clarity over time rather than something that remains implicit, assumed and quietly inconsistent.

# PART FIVE - THE COLD LIST

Everything in the previous section assumed you are building something. That the pipeline is new or at least newly defined and that the focus is on getting enquiries to move forward from this point on.

But some of you are reading this from a different position.

You have been in business long enough to have accumulated something. A database. A CRM. A list of names and conversations and enquiries that came in, started going somewhere and then quietly stopped. Not because those people lost interest necessarily. But because life moved on, the follow-up did not happen at the right moment and the conversation slipped into silence.

That is a different problem. And it deserves its own chapter.

Several of them, actually.

## CHAPTER 12
## COLD IS NOT GONE

There is a version of your database that most business owners never look at directly. Not the active enquiries. Not the recent conversations. The other ones. The ones from three months ago, six months ago, sometimes longer. The people who came in, showed genuine interest, asked real questions and then went quiet.

Most business owners know that part of their database exists. They scroll past it regularly. There is a particular feeling that comes with that scroll, a mixture of mild guilt and mild resignation, as if those conversations represent something that should have gone differently but probably cannot be changed now. So they are left alone. Not deleted. Not addressed. Just left.

Most business owners file those contacts away mentally under the same heading. Done. Not necessarily consciously and not with any formal decision. It just happens. The conversation stops responding and at some point the focus moves to the next enquiry, the next conversation, the next person who is currently showing interest. The quiet ones recede. This is entirely understandable. Attention follows movement. When something stops moving it naturally loses priority. In a business where new enquiries are always arriving there is always something more recent to focus on.

The problem is not that attention moved on. That is a reasonable response to the demands of a working business. The problem is the assumption that quietly formed alongside it. The assumption that quiet means finished. Most of those conversations did not end. They paused. There is a difference and it matters considerably more than it might first appear.

A conversation that ended reached a conclusion. The person decided not to proceed. They found an alternative, the timing did not work, the fit was not right. There was a resolution, even if it was not the one you were hoping for. Something was decided.

A conversation that paused is something else entirely. It simply stopped moving. No decision was made. No alternative was chosen. No door was closed. The momentum was lost, the follow-up did not happen at the right moment and the silence became the default.

From the outside, both look identical. A quiet inbox is a quiet inbox. A contact who has not responded in four months looks the same whether they decided against you or simply got busy and forgot to come back. Without a way to distinguish one from the other, the tendency is to treat them all the same way. And the way most businesses treat them is by leaving them alone.

This is understandable because it feels like the cautious choice. Reaching out to someone who has gone quiet carries a perceived risk of awkwardness. Leaving them alone carries no visible risk at all. The cost of inaction does not show up anywhere. It does not appear in the accounts. It does not trigger a report or generate an alert. It simply sits there, quietly, as the difference between what that enquiry activity could produce and what it currently produces. Which is nothing. Not because the interest was not real. Not because the timing could not work. Not because those people are unreachable. But because no one has gone back to find out.

Over time this becomes a pattern that repeats across most businesses once they have been operating long enough to accumulate a meaningful database. New enquiries receive attention. Recent conversations are managed. The older ones, the ones that went quiet, sit in the background as a kind of commercial archaeology. Present but not active. Acknowledged in theory but not touched in practice. The database grows in one direction and a portion of it settles quietly at the bottom, unexamined and unworked.

## Why Conversations Go Cold

Before addressing what to do about a cold database, it is worth understanding how it got that way. Because it is almost never the result of deliberate neglect. It is the result of recognisable, entirely normal patterns that repeat across most businesses regardless of industry.

The most common reason is simply timing. The enquiry arrived at a moment when the person was genuinely interested but not yet ready to commit. Perhaps they were waiting for a salary review, a season to change, a personal situation to resolve or a conversation with a partner to happen first. When the follow-up stopped, there was nothing to bridge the gap between where they were and where they needed to be to move forward. The window did not close because they decided against it. It closed because nothing kept it open.

A second common reason is response quality in the early stages. An initial message that answered the question without creating a next step left the person with no clear reason to continue. The interaction was technically complete from the business side but incomplete from the buyer's side. They had information but no direction. Over time the conversation faded because there was nothing pulling it forward.

A third reason is the consideration period. Most high-value purchases involve a phase of private evaluation that can last days or weeks. During this period the buyer is not disengaged. They are thinking. They may be discussing the decision with someone, comparing options or simply sitting with it until it feels right. If the pipeline does not maintain contact through that period in a way that feels natural rather than pressured, the conversation loses continuity. The thread breaks. And broken threads are difficult to pick up without an explicit reason to do so.

A fourth reason and perhaps the most quietly significant, is that the business moved on first. A busy period arrived. New enquiries took priority. The older conversations were not deliberately abandoned, they simply received progressively less attention until they were effectively invisible. The buyer may have been ready to continue at a point when no one was there to continue with them.

None of these reasons reflect badly on the business or the buyer. They are structural patterns, predictable consequences of managing enquiries without a pipeline that holds conversations active through their natural duration. Understanding them matters because it changes how the cold database is interpreted. It is not a collection of rejections. It is a collection of conversations that stopped at points where structure could have kept them going.

## What Cold Actually Means

Before going further it is worth being precise about what cold actually means, because the word carries implications that are not always accurate.

Cold suggests distance. It suggests that whatever interest existed has dissipated, cooled and become irrelevant. In some cases that is true. The person has moved on, the need has changed or the moment has passed in a way that cannot be reopened. Some cold contacts are genuinely finished and treating them as recoverable would be a misreading of the situation. But cold is not the same as gone.

In most databases, across most businesses, a meaningful proportion of cold contacts are not cold in the terminal sense. They are cold in the practical sense. The conversation has not been active. The connection has not been maintained. The relationship has not been developed. That is a different condition entirely, because it is a condition that can change.

A cold contact who had genuine interest at the point of enquiry is not the same as a contact who was never interested. The interest existed. Something interrupted the progression. In many cases the interest has not disappeared. It has simply not been given a reason to resurface. The person is not waiting by the phone. They are not thinking about your business daily. But if the right message arrived at the right moment, they might respond. Not because urgency was manufactured or pressure was applied, but because the timing happened to align with where they are now.

The question is not whether those people are still interested. The question is whether anyone has asked. In most cases no one has. The assumption that they were finished was made without testing it and because it was never tested it became permanent by default.

What the Database Actually Contains

Here is where the argument moves from qualitative to quantitative and where most business owners find the shift in perspective most surprising.

Across most businesses, enquiry activity converts within a consistent range under structured conditions. That range varies by industry and by the nature of the purchase decision, but it is measurable and it is predictable.

In jewellery retail, the range tends to sit between 3 and 8 percent of total enquiry volume. In hair clinics it runs between 4 and 10 percent. In med spas between 5 and 12 percent. In cosmetic dental between 5 and 15 percent. These are not arbitrary figures. They reflect the specific combination of buyer intent, consideration cycle, decision weight and pipeline structure that characterises each category. The full reasoning behind each range is worth understanding and that is what the next chapter is built around.

What matters here is the implication of those ranges.

If your business sits at the lower end of the range for your category, the gap between where you are and where a structured pipeline would take you represents a specific and calculable amount of revenue. That gap does not live in the future, waiting to be created by new enquiries. It lives in the existing database, in conversations that started and paused, in contacts who expressed interest and then went quiet while the pipeline moved on without them.

Consider a business receiving 80 enquiries a month with an average transaction value of $3,000. At 3 percent conversion, that produces approximately $7,200 in revenue from enquiry activity each month. At 6 percent, the same volume of enquiries produces approximately $14,400. The enquiries are identical. The value of each transaction is identical. The only variable is how consistently the pipeline carries those conversations toward a conclusion.

The cold database is, in part, the accumulated record of that gap. Not all of it. Some of those contacts were never going to convert regardless of how well the pipeline was managed. But a meaningful portion of them represent conversations that paused at a point where a structured follow-up could have continued them.

The person who enquired about an engagement ring six months ago and went quiet after receiving options may have simply needed more time. The patient who asked about hair treatment after noticing thinning and then stopped responding may have been waiting for the courage to take the next step. The med spa client who asked about lip filler and then retreated may have needed one more message that made the process feel safe enough to continue. The cosmetic dental patient who asked about veneers, received a price range and then went silent may have needed the consultation to be framed as a clarifying step rather than a commitment.

None of these people said no. They paused. And a pause is not the same as a decision.

That is the opportunity sitting inside the database. Not in every contact and not in every cold conversation, but in a proportion that is large enough to represent a number worth calculating, a pattern worth understanding and a conversation worth reopening.

Before that conversation can be approached, it needs to be understood properly. Not in abstract terms, but in terms of what it actually represents in revenue. What those paused interactions are worth if a portion of them were carried through to a conclusion and how that value compares to the way they are currently being treated. That is where the focus moves next.

# CHAPTER 13
# WHAT YOUR COLD LIST IS WORTH

Most business owners have a rough sense of how many enquiries they receive. They know approximately how many conversations are happening at any given time and they have a general feel for how often those conversations turn into business.

What most business owners have never done is apply that same thinking to the enquiries that went cold.

It is a small shift in perspective. Instead of looking only at what has converted, you look at what is sitting in the database that has not converted yet. And instead of assuming those conversations are finished, you treat them as a category with measurable value.

The calculation is not complicated. But before getting to the numbers, it is worth understanding the framework that makes those numbers meaningful. Because the calculation does not work in isolation. It works in relation to a reference point. And that reference point is what enquiry activity should be producing under structured conditions, which varies by industry in ways that are worth understanding clearly.

## What Structured Conversion Actually Looks Like

Across most businesses, enquiry activity converts within a consistent and predictable range when the pipeline is managed well. Not a fixed number, because every business is different and every enquiry environment has its own characteristics. But a range. An observable band of outcomes that reflects what happens when conversations are guided forward rather than left to drift.

That range differs meaningfully across industries and the reasons for those differences are worth understanding because they reveal something important about where the gap between potential and actual performance tends to sit in each category.

In jewellery retail, the conversion range under structured conditions sits between 3 and 8 percent of total enquiry volume, with a midpoint of around 5 percent.

This range reflects the nature of the purchase decision. A jewellery purchase at the mid to high end of the market is considered and emotionally weighted. The buyer is rarely impulse-driven. They are often comparing options, managing a personal timeline and weighing a purchase that carries significance beyond its monetary value. Response time matters significantly in this category. A jewellery enquiry that is answered slowly loses momentum quickly because the emotional readiness present at first contact tends to diminish if the response arrives after the moment has passed. Passive responses, those that answer the question without introducing a next step, are a consistent source of loss. And the consideration cycle, while it may begin quickly, can extend across days or weeks during which the conversation needs to remain active. The gap between the lower and upper ends of the range, roughly 5 percentage points, represents the commercial value of a structured pipeline applied consistently to the same volume of enquiry activity.

In hair clinics, the conversion range under structured conditions sits between 4 and 10 percent of total enquiry volume, with a midpoint of around 7 percent.

This range reflects a buyer who arrives with moderate to high intent but carries a specific type of hesitation that is not present in other categories. Someone reaching out about hair loss has usually been thinking about it for some time before making contact. The enquiry is rarely casual. It represents a decision to acknowledge a concern that is often personal and sometimes emotionally difficult. That same personal dimension creates a consistent pattern of drop-off when the pipeline does not address it directly. The transition from information gathering to consultation introduces a form of commitment that many enquirers pause at. Businesses that handle this transition well, by reducing the perceived commitment involved in taking the next step and by maintaining continuity through the consideration period, see conversion rates toward the upper end of the range. Businesses where the initial response is information-heavy but not outcome-focused tend to lose a higher proportion of enquiries in the early stages.

In med spas, the conversion range under structured conditions sits between 5 and 12 percent of total enquiry volume, with a midpoint of around 8 to 9 percent.

This is a category where the variance in intent at the point of enquiry is higher than in the other three. Some med spa enquiries arrive from people who are effectively ready to book and are simply confirming a detail before doing so. Others arrive from people who are curious and somewhat self-conscious about the enquiry itself and who will disengage quickly if the initial interaction does not feel comfortable and normalising. That self-consciousness creates a specific and fast-closing window. An enquiry that is met with a warm, specific and outcome-focused response tends to move forward. One that receives a generic or purely informational response tends to go quiet quickly and is difficult to re-engage from that position. Businesses that address the self-consciousness dimension effectively in their initial response and that frame the consultation as a low-commitment clarifying step rather than a formal commitment, consistently see conversion rates toward the upper end of the range.

In cosmetic dental, the conversion range under structured conditions sits between 5 and 15 percent of total enquiry volume, with a midpoint of around 10 percent.

This is the widest range of the four categories and that width is not accidental. It reflects the fact that the gap between a well-managed pipeline and a poorly managed one is larger here than anywhere else, because the treatment value is higher, the consideration cycle is longer and the decision carries more weight. Intent at the point of enquiry tends to be high. A person asking about veneers or a smile makeover has generally been considering it for some time. That level of intent creates a strong starting position. But the decision involves multiple dimensions that must be addressed in sequence for conversion to occur reliably. Cost, timing, desired outcome, process and confidence in the result all factor in, often simultaneously and must each be navigated through a pipeline that maintains continuity across what can be a lengthy consideration period. Businesses that manage this well, guiding the enquiry through each dimension rather than moving quickly to consultation before context is established and following up consistently after the consultation through the decision period, tend to see conversion rates toward the upper end. Businesses where the pipeline loses continuity during the consideration period tend to sit toward the lower end regardless of how well the initial interaction was handled.

Understanding these ranges matters because it changes what the cold database represents.

## The Calculation

If your business is operating toward the lower end of the range for your category, the gap between where you are and where a structured pipeline would take you represents a specific and calculable amount of revenue. And a portion of that gap lives not in future enquiries but in the existing database, in conversations that started and paused before the pipeline had the opportunity to carry them through.

The calculation that makes this visible starts with three numbers.

The first is volume. How many contacts in your database went quiet without reaching a decision? Not the total database size and not all historical contacts, but specifically the ones who expressed genuine interest, had at least one meaningful interaction and then stopped progressing. In most businesses that have been operating for more than a year, this number is larger than expected.

The second is value. What is the average value of a piece of business in your category? A sale, a project, a contract, a treatment. Whatever the unit of revenue looks like for your business, what does it typically represent in dollar terms?

The third is rate. Of the cold contacts who are re-engaged in a structured way, what proportion typically respond and progress? This is not conversion to sale. It is simply the proportion who re-enter a conversation. The re-engagement rate tends to sit within a range that reflects the same industry dynamics described above, though it is typically more conservative than the initial conversion range because some of those contacts have genuinely moved on in the time since their original enquiry.

When those three numbers are analysed together, something happens that tends to surprise business owners who go through this exercise for the first time. The database starts to look less like a graveyard and more like a pipeline that has not been activated yet.

Seeing the Number

Most business owners, when they calculate this for the first time, experience a version of the same reaction. First, mild scepticism. The number seems too large. It feels unlikely that this much potential is sitting in a database they have been managing for months or years without realising it.

Then, a slower recalibration. Because the number is not speculative. It is derived from their own enquiry volume, their own average transaction value and a realistic re-engagement rate applied to their own category. It is not optimistic. It is a reasonable estimate of what that activity represents if a structured approach is applied to it.

And then, usually, a quiet version of a familiar question: 'Why has nobody ever shown me this before?'

The honest answer is that most of the attention in most businesses flows toward new activity. New enquiries. New conversations. New opportunities. The existing database is managed reactively rather than proactively. It is a record of what has happened rather than a resource to be worked. Once the number is visible, that tends to change.

Not all of it is recoverable. That is worth stating clearly. Some of those contacts have genuinely moved on. The need has changed, the timing has passed or the decision was made in favour of someone else during the period of silence. Those conversations are finished and treating them as recoverable would be a misreading of the situation.

But some will respond. And the proportion that will is almost always larger than the proportion that has been tested, because in most cases the proportion that has been tested is close to zero. The assumption that those contacts are finished was made without testing it and it became permanent simply because no one went back to find out.

## What This Number Represents

This is not theoretical revenue. It is not a projection built on wishful thinking or optimistic assumptions. It is an estimate of the commercial value sitting in conversations that already happened, with people who already showed interest, in a business that has already done the work of attracting them.

The cost of generating those enquiries has already been paid. Whether that cost was advertising spend, time, networking, referrals or reputation, it was incurred at the point of original enquiry. The return on that cost was partial. A conversation started. The conversation stopped. The question is whether the remaining value can be accessed.

Consider a business receiving 60 enquiries a month in a category where structured conversion sits at a midpoint of around 7 percent. At 3 percent conversion, that business is producing roughly $12,600 in revenue from enquiry activity each month, assuming an average transaction value of $7,000. At 7 percent, the same volume produces roughly $29,400. The enquiries are identical. The transaction value is identical. The only variable is how consistently the pipeline carries those conversations toward a conclusion.

Over twelve months, that difference on the same enquiry volume becomes a number that is difficult to forget once you've discovered it.

The cold database is, in significant part, the accumulated record of that gap. Not all of it, because some loss is inevitable in any pipeline. But enough of it to make the calculation worth doing and the re-engagement worth attempting. That is what the cold list is worth. Not a vague sense of untapped potential. A number. Derived from your own volume, your own average value and a realistic rate applied to your specific category. Once that number is visible, the next question is straightforward. What do you do with it? That is what the next chapter addresses.

# CHAPTER 14
# SWITCHING THE CONVERSATIONS BACK ON

Re-engaging a cold contact is not the same as starting from scratch.

That distinction is worth holding onto, because the instinct when approaching a cold database is almost always to treat it like a new outreach exercise. A new message is written. A new introduction is made. Interest is sought again from the beginning as if the previous interaction never happened. That approach misunderstands what a cold contact actually represents.

A cold contact is not a stranger. They are someone who, at a previous point in time, found your business relevant enough to make contact. They asked a question, requested information or started a conversation. That interaction happened. It is part of the history between you. And that history has value, because it establishes a prior connection and gives the re-engagement something to build from rather than something to overcome.

The starting point is not introduction. It is continuation.

This changes everything about how the message is written. Not in an obvious or dramatic way, but in a way that the person receiving it can feel even if they cannot name it. A message that treats them as a stranger creates a small but real friction. It asks them to start again from the beginning of a process they already began. A message that treats them as someone who was previously in a conversation, even a brief one, asks considerably less of them. It invites them back into something that already exists rather than asking them to initiate something new.

## Understanding the Person on the Other End

Before thinking about what to write, it is worth thinking about who is receiving the message and what their experience of the situation actually is.

In most cases, the cold contact is not thinking about the business at all. They are not sitting with a lingering sense of guilt about not responding. They are not weighing up whether to re-engage. They are simply living their life, in which the conversation that happened some months ago occupies no active space. The original interest was real. The circumstances that surrounded it have moved on. The question is not whether they can be reached. It is whether something in the message creates enough relevance in their present moment to produce a response.

This matters because it changes the job of the re-engagement message entirely. The message is not trying to remind someone of something they have been meaning to do. It is trying to create a small moment of recognition, a sense that this is relevant to something they care about, right now, in the context of where they are today rather than where they were when the original enquiry happened.

Some contacts will respond quickly because the message arrives at exactly the right moment. The original interest never fully disappeared. The circumstances that prevented them from moving forward have changed. The message gave them a reason to act on something they had been half-intending to return to anyway.

Others will respond after a second or third message, not because the first one failed, but because the timing simply was not aligned at that moment. The seed was planted. A subsequent message found the moment.

And some will not respond at all. The situation has genuinely changed, the need has passed or the decision was made elsewhere during the period of silence. That is a normal and expected outcome and it should not colour how the process is approached. Not every re-engagement produces a response. The point is that enough of them do to make the exercise consistently worthwhile.

## What the Message Needs to Do

A well-constructed re-engagement message does three things. It acknowledges the prior contact without over-explaining it. It creates a reason to respond that is relevant in the present moment rather than tied only to what happened before. And it makes responding feel easy rather than like a commitment that requires effort to process.

The tone sits between familiar and introductory, because that is where the relationship actually sits. Not close enough to assume intimacy. Not distant enough to pretend there was no previous connection. The message reflects the reality of what exists between the two parties, which is a conversation that started and did not finish.

Consider the difference between these two approaches for a jewellery retail context.

The first message reads: "Hi, just checking in to see if you are still looking for an engagement ring."

The second reads: "Hi, just checking whether the solitaire options I sent through were close to what you had in mind or whether it would help to look at something a bit different."

Both messages are short. Both are polite. But the second one does something the first does not. It refers to a specific detail of the previous interaction, which signals that the person was remembered as an individual rather than as a name on a list. It also asks a specific, easy-to-answer question rather than a general one that requires the person to reconstruct context before they can respond. That difference, which looks small on the surface, produces meaningfully different outcomes across a database at volume.

The Sequence

Re-engagement is not a single message. It is a short sequence, spaced over time, where each message performs a slightly different function while maintaining a consistent tone.

The first message reintroduces contact in a light and proportionate way. It references the prior interaction, creates a simple and specific reason to respond and does not attempt to move immediately to a decision. Its job is simply to reopen the channel without creating friction.

If there is no response, the second message approaches from a different angle. It is not a copy of the first message with different wording. It is a separate attempt to find the moment. It may frame the situation differently, ask a different kind of question or introduce something specific that creates a fresh reason to respond. The underlying purpose is the same but the approach is distinct enough that it does not feel like repetition.

If a third message is needed, it is often the shortest and the most direct. It acknowledges that the timing may not be right and leaves the door open without applying any pressure at all. Something like: "No pressure at all. If the timing has changed or things have moved in a different direction, that is completely fine. Just let me know if you would like to pick this up again at any point." In many cases, responses arrive at this third message not despite its brevity but because of it. There is nothing to resist. The message removes all expectation from the act of replying and that removal is sometimes exactly what is needed.

After this sequence, the contact is not discarded. It is simply recognised that the current timing is not aligned. The conversation can be revisited later at an appropriate interval. What it should not become is repeated interruption, which erodes goodwill and closes doors permanently rather than leaving them open.

### What Re-engagement Is Not

Because re-engagement is sometimes confused with approaches that produce the opposite of the intended result, it is worth being direct about what it is not.

It is not a broadcast. Sending the same generic message to an entire database without regard for the context of each individual interaction is not re-engagement. It is volume outreach. The response rates reflect that and more importantly the quality of the responses reflects it. A message that treats someone as a number on a list produces a response, if it produces one at all, from someone who feels like a number on a list.

It is not pressure. Introducing urgency, limited availability or any form of manufactured scarcity is not creating relevance. It is creating noise. In the context of a cold contact who has already experienced a conversation that faded without conclusion, a pressured message is not a reason to re-engage. It is a reason to disengage permanently.

It is not a reminder of absence. Drawing attention to how long it has been or framing the message around the fact that there has been no contact for some time, does not give the person a reason to respond.

It creates mild awkwardness that they have to navigate rather than a reason to continue. The gap in the conversation does not need to be explained or apologised for. It simply needs to be bridged.

## What Happens When It Works

When re-engagement is applied well across a meaningful volume of cold contacts, something observable begins to happen.

Conversations that were effectively invisible start to reappear in the pipeline. Not all at once and not in every case, but steadily and consistently. Some contacts respond to the first message. Others respond to the second or third. A proportion does not respond at all and those are recognised as having genuinely concluded rather than being pursued beyond what the interaction supports.

What changes is the relationship between the database and the pipeline. The database is no longer purely a historical record of what happened and went quiet. It becomes a resource that is actively worked, a pipeline that has not been fully activated yet rather than a graveyard of lost opportunities.

The contacts who re-engage do not return to the beginning of the process. They return to somewhere in the middle, where context already exists and a decision has simply not yet been reached. Treating them as new enquiries removes the advantage of everything that was already established. Treating them as continuations preserves it and makes the path to a conclusion considerably shorter.

This is where re-engagement begins to function as something more than a tactic. It becomes a consistent and repeatable source of pipeline activity that runs alongside the management of new enquiries rather than replacing it. A steady stream of previously cold conversations being reactivated, a proportion of which progress and some of which reach a conclusion. That is what makes it worth building into a system rather than treating as a one-off exercise. Which is exactly what the next chapter is about.

# CHAPTER 15
# MAKING RE-ENGAGEMENT REPEATABLE

The most common mistake businesses make with re-engagement is treating it as a one-off exercise.

Something triggers it. A slow month, a conversation about what is sitting in the database, a moment of clarity about how much enquiry activity has quietly accumulated without reaching a conclusion. A decision is made to go back through the cold list. Messages are sent. Some responses come in. A number of conversations restart. The exercise produces something visible and for a brief period it feels like the problem has been addressed.

Then it stops.

The database returns to its previous state. New enquiries arrive, receive attention and over time a proportion of them join the existing group of cold contacts in the part of the database that is no longer actively managed. The cycle repeats. The gap between what the business could be producing and what it actually produces remains in place, not because the opportunity is not there but because the way it is handled has not fundamentally changed.

This is not a failure of re-engagement as a concept. It is a consequence of how it was applied. When it is treated as an event, it produces event-like outcomes. A short period of activity followed by a return to baseline. When it is treated as a process, it produces something different altogether.

## Why a System Behaves Differently from an Event

A database is not static. It is constantly growing in one direction. Every week, new enquiries come in. Some convert immediately. Some take longer. Others begin to move and then pause at a point where the next step was not defined or the follow-up did not arrive at the right moment. Without a structured way of revisiting those paused interactions, they accumulate quietly at the bottom of the database while attention flows consistently toward whatever is newest and most visible.

The feeling of scrolling past that accumulated section is familiar to most business owners who have been operating for more than a year. There is a version of that scroll where it produces mild guilt and resignation, a sense that those contacts represent something that should have gone differently but probably cannot be changed now. That feeling is partly what keeps the database unworked. Re-engaging a contact from six months ago feels presumptuous. Leaving them alone feels safer.

A repeatable re-engagement process changes what that scroll looks like. Not because the contacts are different, but because each one now has a defined place in a structure that is actively managing them. Some have been through the first message. Some are waiting for the second. Some have responded and are back in the active pipeline. Some have been recognised as genuinely concluded and noted accordingly. The database is no longer a record of things that happened and stopped. It is a system in motion.

That shift is not dramatic. It does not announce itself. But over time it changes the character of the business in ways that become visible in the numbers.

## What a Repeatable Process Actually Looks Like

In practice, a repeatable re-engagement process does not require revisiting the entire database at once. That approach is both impractical and counterproductive. It produces a burst of activity that cannot be sustained and sets up the same event-based pattern that causes the problem in the first place. What it requires instead is consistency in how smaller portions of the database are handled at regular intervals.

At a defined point in the week, a segment of cold contacts is selected and moved through the re-engagement sequence. The segment might be based on when the conversation went quiet, perhaps contacts who have been inactive for between three and six months represent the most productive starting point in most businesses. It might be based on the stage the conversation reached before stopping, contacts who progressed further into the pipeline before going cold often have a higher rate of re-engagement than those who dropped off early. Or it might be based on the type of enquiry, prioritising the categories with the highest average transaction value first.

The segment moves through the sequence. Responses are recorded. Conversations that restart are returned to the active pipeline and managed from the point they had previously reached. Contacts who do not respond are noted and scheduled to be revisited at a later interval rather than being left to accumulate indefinitely or discarded prematurely.

This process takes less time than most business owners expect once it is established. The decisions about what to say are already made. The sequence already exists. The only variable is which contacts are being moved through it in any given week. Once the rhythm is in place it becomes simply part of how the business operates, something that happens consistently rather than something that requires a separate decision to initiate.

The parallel to what was discussed in Chapter 8 is direct. Repeatability fails not in design but in application and it fails most reliably when it depends on finding spare time or on remembering what needs to happen rather than having a structure that makes the next action visible. The re-engagement process faces exactly the same risk. If it requires a conscious decision to begin each time, it will happen inconsistently. If it is integrated into the regular rhythm of the working week, it will happen reliably.

## What Changes Over Time

When re-engagement is applied consistently over a longer period, the behaviour of the database begins to shift in a way that is gradual but observable.

Cold contacts are not left to accumulate in the same way because they are revisited before they become too distant. The proportion that responds remains more stable because the timing of re-engagement is more consistent. In most businesses, contacts who are re-engaged within six months of going cold respond at a higher rate than those left for longer, simply because the context of the original conversation is still more accessible and the circumstances of the person's life are less likely to have changed significantly.

The outcome is not a spike of recovered activity. It is a steady stream of previously inactive conversations being reintroduced into the pipeline. Some of those conversations progress. Some reach a conclusion. Some are recognised as genuinely finished and treated accordingly. What changes is that the process continues to produce these outcomes over time rather than producing them once in response to a slow month and then stopping. That is the difference between re-engagement as an event and re-engagement as a system. An event produces a temporary shift. A system produces an ongoing pattern of behaviour that can be observed, measured and relied upon.

## Bringing Both Parts Together

At this point it is worth stepping back and looking at what the two sections of this book describe when they are considered together, because the connection between them is the most important thing to take from it.

The first section was about building structure within active enquiry flow. Defining the stages of the pipeline, aligning messaging to each stage, creating next steps that carry conversations forward rather than leaving them to drift and maintaining that structure consistently under normal working conditions. That work establishes the forward movement of the pipeline. New demand comes in and is carried through a defined process toward a conclusion.

The second section has been about something complementary. It takes the enquiries that entered that process but did not reach a conclusion and gives them another path. Not a second chance in the sentimental sense, but a structured reintroduction into the same system that handles everything else. Re-engagement does not create new demand. It works with demand that has already been generated, partially processed and then paused before completion.

When both parts are operating together, something useful happens to the system as a whole.

New enquiries enter and are carried forward with structure. Paused enquiries are revisited and given another opportunity to progress.

The database stops being divided into an active section and a dormant section and starts behaving as a single managed resource. Conversations move forward, pause, return and reach conclusions over time rather than being left at the point where they happened to stop.

Fewer interactions are assumed complete when they are actually just quiet. Fewer are allowed to drift indefinitely simply because no structure exists to bring them back. More reach a defined conclusion, whether that conclusion is a conversion or a genuine decision not to proceed. And both of those outcomes are more useful than the third option, which is simply disappearing.

This is not a complicated system. It does not require significant changes to how the business operates. It does not depend on new technology or expensive infrastructure. What it requires is consistency in how conversations are carried, whether they are new or returning and a structure that makes that consistency possible under real working conditions rather than ideal ones.

When that consistency is present, the relationship between enquiry activity and revenue outcome becomes more stable and more predictable. A good month is no longer the result of an unusually strong week of new enquiries. A slow month is no longer explained entirely by a drop in inbound activity. The pipeline is producing movement at multiple points simultaneously. New conversations are progressing. Older ones are being reactivated. The full range of existing demand is being worked rather than a fraction of it.

That is the point at which the system described across both sections of this book stops being a concept and becomes the actual operating structure of the business.

A business that treats enquiries as individual interactions, to be managed in the moment and left when attention moves elsewhere, produces outcomes that reflect that approach. Variable, difficult to predict and heavily dependent on which conversations happened to receive the right attention at the right time.

A business that treats enquiries as part of a continuous system, one that carries them forward when they arrive and brings them back when they pause, produces outcomes that reflect something different. More consistent, more closely aligned with the level of demand that actually exists and considerably less dependent on any single conversation going well. That is not a small distinction. It is the difference between a business that generates revenue and a business that produces it.

# CONCLUSION
# THE SYSTEM WAS ALWAYS THERE

You did not come to this book because business was going badly.

You came because something did not quite add up. Enquiries were arriving. Conversations were happening. Some of them were converting. But the results felt inconsistent in a way that was difficult to explain and even harder to fix, because nothing was obviously broken and there was no single moment to point to as the problem.

That feeling is the most accurate diagnosis available. Not a failure of effort or talent or product. A gap between what the activity should be producing and what it actually is. A gap that exists not because the demand is missing but because the system that was supposed to carry that demand through to a conclusion was not quite doing its job.

That is what this book has been about.

Not a new idea. Not a methodology invented in a boardroom and applied to businesses from the outside. A pattern that already exists inside every business that handles enquiries, made visible so that it can be understood, adjusted and used deliberately rather than experienced passively.

The pipeline is not something you build and add to your business. It is already there. It is the sequence your enquiries travel from the moment they arrive to the moment a decision is made. What the book has described is how to make that sequence intentional. How to see where it slows. How to understand why some conversations progress and others do not. And how to apply structure consistently enough that the movement becomes reliable rather than occasional.

The same applies to the conversations that have already taken place and gone quiet. Those are not failures. Most of them are not even decisions. They are pauses. Points where the momentum was lost, the follow-up did not arrive at the right moment and the silence filled in where a next step should have been. Re-engagement is not about recovering losses. It is about returning to conversations that were not actually finished and giving them another path forward.

Together, those two things, carrying new enquiries forward and returning to the ones that paused, form a complete view of the commercial activity that already exists inside your business. Not the activity that might exist if marketing improves or if the product changes or if circumstances become more favourable. The activity that is already there right now, in the inbox and the CRM and the database of contacts who expressed interest and then went quiet while the business moved on without them.

That activity is worth more than most business owners realise. Not in a vague, motivational sense. In a specific, calculable sense. Based on enquiry volume, average transaction value and a realistic conversion range derived from the industry you operate in. That number is knowable. And once it is known, it is difficult to look at without wanting to do something about it.

Here is the part this book cannot do for you.

It cannot apply the structure on your behalf. It cannot maintain the consistency when the week gets busy and the inbox gets full and the easier thing is to focus on what is newest and most visible. It cannot revisit the cold contacts when they have been sitting untouched for six months and the assumption that they are finished has had time to feel true.

That part is yours.

And it is harder than understanding the concept. Not because the tasks are complicated. They are not. But because consistency under real working conditions is always harder than consistency in principle. The pipeline that functions well in a calm week starts to slip in a busy one. The re-engagement sequence that was built with good intentions gets delayed when something more urgent arrives. The structure that was designed to make movement automatic starts to require manual effort again and manual effort is always in shorter supply than anyone plans for.

This is not a reason to abandon the system. It is a reason to build it in a way that does not depend on ideal conditions to function. Simple stages. Clear next steps. A re-engagement rhythm that is small enough to be sustainable rather than ambitious enough to be aspirational. A process that can be applied on an ordinary Wednesday afternoon when there are six other things competing for attention, not just on the Monday morning when everything feels possible.

The businesses that produce revenue consistently are not doing something dramatically different from the ones that produce it occasionally. They have made the same process more reliable. That is all. The conversations are similar. The enquiries are similar. The effort is similar. What differs is how consistently the structure holds under the conditions that actually exist.

That consistency is available to any business that decides to build it.

What changes when it is in place is not dramatic on any given day. A conversation is followed up that might otherwise have been left. A cold contact receives a message that brings them back into a conversation they had not quite finished. A paused enquiry is revisited before it disappears permanently. None of those moments feel like turning points in the moment. Across a month, across a quarter, across a year, they accumulate into something that is visible and real and considerably more closely aligned with what the existing level of activity is capable of producing.

That is the shift. Not from bad to good, but from inconsistent to reliable.

Revenue stops being something that happens to the business and starts being something the business produces. On purpose. Through a system that was always there, waiting to be made visible and used.

If you would like to find out what your current enquiry activity should be producing in revenue, the calculation is straightforward and it starts with three numbers. You can request it at soliswebtech.com/calculation-request and I will come back to you with what the number looks like for your specific business. That is where it starts.

# THE NEXT STEP

Something brought you to this book. A suspicion that the enquiry activity in your business is not producing what it should. A pattern of inconsistent results that felt structural rather than accidental. A sense that somewhere between the conversations that are happening and the revenue that is appearing, something is being lost.

That suspicion is almost certainly correct.

Most businesses have never mapped what their existing enquiry activity should be producing in revenue terms. Not in theory, not as an aspiration, but as a specific number derived from their own volume, their own average transaction value and a realistic conversion range for the category they operate in.

Without that number, performance is difficult to interpret. A strong month and a slow month can look similar on the surface. Conversations are happening. Some outcomes are being achieved. What is missing is a reference point that makes the difference between the two months visible and explainable.

That is what the calculation provides.

It does not require access to your systems. It does not require a change to how you generate enquiries. It takes three numbers that already exist within your business and applies them in a structured way to produce a range that represents what your current enquiry activity is capable of producing when it is consistently carried through.

For some businesses, that number confirms that the current process is broadly aligned with what is possible. For others, it reveals a gap that is larger than expected. Not because something dramatic is wrong, but because small variations have been compounding quietly over time without ever being measured.

Seeing the number changes how decisions are made.

It shifts the focus from increasing activity to understanding how existing activity is actually performing. It provides a clear reference point for evaluating whether conversations are being carried through effectively and whether the pipeline is functioning as a system or as a collection of individual interactions that depend on memory and timing to produce results.

If the ideas in this book have felt familiar, the next step is straightforward.

Take your current enquiry volume. Take your average transaction value. Take a realistic sense of how many of those enquiries go cold before a decision is made.

I will tell you what that activity should be producing.

The calculation is free and it takes about three minutes on my end.

You can request it at soliswebtech.com/calculation-request.

# ABOUT THE AUTHOR

I did not set out to write a book about sales pipelines.

I came to this work through a much longer path. More than three decades across marketing, lead generation, copywriting and conversion, building funnels, managing enquiry flow and writing copy across industries including health, jewellery and weight management. Most of that work involved not only attracting demand but handling what happened after demand arrived. And the longer I did it, the harder it became to ignore a pattern that kept repeating across different businesses in different categories.

The businesses I worked with were not short of enquiries. They were short of a consistent way of carrying those enquiries through to a conclusion. The activity was present. The outcomes were not matching it. And in most cases, nobody had ever measured the gap because it did not present itself as a failure. It looked like normal variation.

That observation became the foundation of Solis, where I shifted focus from generating activity to analysing and structuring how existing enquiry pipelines were actually performing. What I found, consistently, was that a meaningful portion of potential revenue was sitting inside conversations that had already happened but had not been carried through. Not because the opportunity was not there. Because no system existed to take it there.

This book is drawn from that work. Not from a single methodology applied from the outside, but from patterns observed across many businesses, over time, in real operating environments where things get busy and structures break down and the gap between understanding what needs to happen and actually having it happen is wider than anyone plans for.

I know that gap well. I have lived on both sides of it.

Outside of this work I am most grounded in the things that do not involve screens or spreadsheets. I have four adult children and two grandchildren who collectively keep me honest about what actually matters. I have dogs who require walking regardless of what the inbox looks like. And I have a vegetable garden that produces more than I can eat and demands nothing except consistent attention, which turns out to be the same thing a good pipeline requires.

That last part is not a metaphor I planned. It just turned out to be true.

If you would like to continue the conversation, I am at soliswebtech.com

www.ingramcontent.com/pod-product-compliance
Lightning Source LLC
LaVergne TN
LVHW010624100826
845148LV00014B/3102
* 9 7 8 1 7 6 4 1 9 8 0 2 8 *